YOGIC CURE FOR COMMON DISEASES

Learn-it-Yourself Books are specially designed to enable the readers to learn useful skills and techniques, and obtain sound, authoritative information of value in their professional, family and personal lives.

The subjects of these books have been selected on the criterion of their utility for a large number of readers. The books are comprehensive and, in some cases, are designed as workbooks to serve the readers as self-learning guides.

This is an important book because it for the first time deals with the yogic cures for various human diseases in such detail. The author who is the founder-director of the Institute of Yoga at Patna and Washington has wide experience in this particular aspect of yogic culture. He has treated many at his institute, and written a number of books on yoga. In this book he discusses diseases ranging from Indigestion to Arthritis and Heart Ailments to Neck & Spinal Pain and suggests suitable cures for them through the practice of yoga.

"Asanas are described simply... and plenty of illustrations act as exact guides. A book which will help a patient in treating himself."

Hindustan Times

"Many common ailments can be cured or alleviated by following the clear instructions given in the book."

Times of India

YOGIC CURE
FOR
COMMON DISEASES

Dr. Phulgenda Sinha
Director
Indian Institute of Yoga,
Patna, India & Washington, USA.

**Orient
Paperbacks**
DELHI | MUMBAI | HYDERABAD

To
My Wife,
Shanti Devi

www.orientpaperbacks.com

ISBN 81-222-0035-4

1st Published 1976
Revised Enlarged Edition 1980
18th Printing 2005

Yogic Cure for Common Diseases

© Phulgenda Sinha, 1976

Cover design by Vision Studio

Published by
Orient Paperbacks
(A Division of Vision Books Pvt. Ltd.)
5A/8 Ansari Road, New Delhi-110 002

Printed in India at
Jay Kay Offset Printers, Delhi-110 041

Cover Printed at
Ravindra Printing Press, Delhi-110 006

Preface

It has given me immense pleasure to read letters of appreciation on the low-cost edition of *Yogic Cure for Common Diseases*. People not only from India, but also from countries of Asia and Europe have spoken very highly of my contribution in the field of Therapeutic Yoga. I have felt highly honoured.

In the low-cost edition, I had purposely limited the coverage to only eight chapters in order to keep the book in a moderate size. But ever since its publication, a good number of people have requested me to cover some more common ailments and disorders of which I have the experience of treating and curing. Considering these requests, I have enlarged this and added four new chapters in this edition. Chapter 8 covers Neck and Spinal Pain, Chapter 9 is on Sinus and Headache, Chapter 10 shows the yogic method of curing Eye Disorders and Chapter 12 provides a Chart of Daily Yoga Practice for maintaining good health. I am sure, these additions would make the book more useful to the people.

Phulgenda Sinha

Contents

Note: The text and illustrations have been given separately. The numbers in the text relate to the illustrations which are serially numbered. For example (1 and 2) means illustrations 1 and 2 appearing on page 49, and further.

List of Illustrations

1

Therapeutic Yoga And
Its Essentials

THERAPEUTIC YOGA is basically a system of self-treatment. According to yogic view, diseases, disorders and ailments are the result of faulty ways of living, bad habits, lack of proper knowledge of things related to individual's life, and improper food. The diseases are thus the resultant state of a short or prolonged malfunctioning of the body system. This malfunctioning is caused by an imbalanced internal condition, created due to certain errors of the individuals.

Since the root cause of a disease lies in the mistakes of the individual, its cure also lies in correcting those mistakes by the same individual. Thus, it is the individual himself who is responsible in both the cases, that is, for causing as well as for curing the disease.

This being the basic assumption in this system about the nature of the trouble and its remedy, there is total reliance on the effort of the patient himself. The yoga expert shows only the path and works no more than as a counsellor to the patient.

The yogic process of treatment comprises three steps: (i) Proper diet, (ii) Proper yoga practice, and (iii) Proper knowledge of things which concern the life of an individual. By following these steps, a disease is cured.[1] A brief description of these steps is provided below:

Proper Diet

The diet is recommended according to the nature of the disease and the condition of the patient. The main idea about diet is to keep it balanced and at the same time eliminate those items from the daily intake which are considered harmful in case of a particular disease. A diet-chart for breakfast, lunch, afternoon refreshment, and the dinner is prepared for each patient according to his body condition and the nature of his disease.

The most common items of diet for almost all patients of therapeutic yoga are: fruits, salad, leafy vegetables, green vegetables, wheat bread and pulses (selected). For non-vegetarians, fish and liver are allowed in certain cases but meat and chicken are generally forbidden. Whatever be the variations in the diet-chart of patients, all of them are asked to follow some basic principles of eating which means: to eat slowly, to eat only 85 per cent of the capacity, to eat at least two hours before their retiring time at night, to avoid drinking water while eating, not to eat hot, spicy, fried and roasted food, not to take more than one or two cups of coffee or tea in a day and if possible to stop these completely, to give up the use of tobacco in any form, and to avoid the use of alcohol.

Yoga Practice

The patient is asked to practise yoga according to his disease and his bodily conditions. In a majority of the cases, a regular practice of only a few *asanas* is enough for

---

[1]The diseases referred to here are specially the chronic type. We do not know as yet if yoga therapy can cure all sorts of communicable diseases such as, venereal diseases (V.D.), pox and similar others, though the occurrence of even these diseases can be prevented by yoga practice.

12

curing the diseases. In some of the diseases the practice of *pranayama* together with the *asanas* becomes essential for good results. In certain cases, specific *kriyas* such as *bandhas, mudras* and certain yogic techniques are used for the desired result. Besides these, practice of concentration and meditation is also necessary in certain cases.

In our research at the Indian Institute of Yoga, Patna, we have found that a large number of diseases are cured within two months of yoga practice. In certain cases, it takes about four months or even more. Diseases that take a longer time are juvenile diabetes, polio, paralysis, parkinsonism, obesity, ulcer, mental health cases, etc.

It is interesting to note that the same *asanas, pranayamas, bandhas, mudras,* and other *kriyas* which are practised for creative, preventive and general health purposes are practised also for curing diseases. But there is a difference in the manner of practice by a patient and by a general practitioner. The patient of a particular disease is advised to practise only as much of an *asana* as is possible for him.

By doing only what is physically performable, the patient gains in strength as the *kriyas* begin to condition the body and diminish the disease. When the disease is cured, physical ability improves and the same *asanas* are performed better even by those who were unable to do them at the beginning.

The yoga therapy is a specialised form of yogic culture and various yoga centres in India have developed their own systems on the basis of their experience and research. In the absence of any standardisation, there is some variation in the method of therapeutic yoga at various centres in India and elsewhere.[2]

---

[2]For understanding the variation in this process of therapeutic yoga, see the following sources: *Yoga Mimansa,* a quarterly journal of Kaivalyadhama, Lonavla (Poona); *Yoga,* a monthly journal of the Vishwayatan Yogashram, New Delhi; *Yoga,* annual publication of the Institute of Yoga, Patna.

Proper Knowledge

Though most of the patients are cured with only proper diet ar d yoga practice, there are some cases which are complicated. Some patients develop diseases and disorders on account of their false assumptions, unhealthy habits, and lack of proper knowledge about life, nature and society.

In such cases, a lot of things need to be told to the patient which are informative, conceptual, theoretical and also philosophical. It is a time-consuming work. Yogic literature is very rich in this respect and is divided into two main categories: (i) spiritual interpretation of things, and (ii) scientific interpretation of things. However, the literature available in the second category is much less than that in the first one. The readers are best advised to have a scientific approach in all their reading on yoga.[3] Depending upon the nature of disease, a patient is counselled and informed in detail about the various concerned aspects of life.

With this short description about the method of therapeutic yoga, we now explain how it differs from the medical system of treatment.

Yoga vs. Medical System

In any medical system the primary reliance is on medicine. It is assumed that a particular medicine will cure a particular disease. The medical doctor does the diagnosis, identifies the disease and prescribes a suitable medicine. The patient in this system has to do very little or nothing at all. The task of correcting the disease and disorder and restoring health is assigned to the medicine.

Seen in this context, there is a contrast between the

---

[3]Pertinent literature: Swami Vivekanand, *Jnana and Karma Yoga;* Kapil, *Samkhya Darshan;* Swami Sivanand, *Thought Power;* Swami Kuvalayananda, *Pranayam;* Yogendra, *Yoga Essays;* and Dr. Phulgenda Sinha, *Yoga: Meaning, Values and Practice.*

medical system and yogic system of treatment. Whereas in the medical system an external agent (medicine) does the corrective work, in the yogic system this external agent is not needed at all. As said earlier, it is the patient himself whose personal understanding, practice and care cures his disease in the yogic system.

It would not be improper to mention that we encountered several patients suffering from various chronic diseases, who had lost their faith in the medical system because inspite of years of treatment they had not achieved permanent and satisfactory cure. In certain cases, the medicine provided them immediate relief, but not a lasting cure. On the other hand, a great number of such patients achieved permanent cure through therapeutic yoga within a period of two to four months. This has specially been so in cases of diabetes, arthritis, asthma, gastro-intestinal disorders, nervous tension and various other cases.

This limitation of the medical system should not mean that it is inferior to the yoga system; rather it is only a matter of the limitation and scope of a given system. There are areas where only the medical science and not yoga can come to the rescue of the patient. Similarly, there are certain diseases, which though regarded incurable through medicinal system, are definitely cured through yoga. This shows that every system of treatment has certain unique points as well as limitations.

Further, the medical treatment has now become so expensive that millions of people all over the world cannot afford it. It is, therefore, not surprising that our hospitals now fail to provide medicines to the patients although they used to do so liberally in the past. Yoga on the other hand does not involve any expenses.

Therefore, it would be prudent on the part of the medical men to adopt and use this tested ancient system of yoga for treating those diseases and ailments whose medicinal cure is not certain. Since the system of therapeutic yoga is now scientifically established, it can be used as a 'self-cure method' by people suffering from various disorders in any part of the world. Let me now explain its essentials which one must know for making proper use of therapeutic yoga.

Essentials of Yoga Practice

Readers who would use this book as a guide for 'self-treatment through yoga' need first to be told about the suitability of time, place, body condition, dress and similar other matters. In order to derive full benefit of therapeutic yoga it is necessary to understand the following requirements and principles related to its practice:

Time

Though the morning time, before breakfast, is regarded best for practising yoga, one can do it also in the evening or at any other time, provided the stomach is empty and not heavy with food. The general principle is to give an interval of three to four hours after eating and then do yoga. Also a gap of half an hour or so should be given after drinking water, tea or any juice. The body should be in a restful and normal condition at the time of practising yoga.

The individual should select a time which is convenient for his daily routine and should *try to do yoga at the same time every day*. A practice for at least five to six days in a week should be enough to show improvement. The patients are advised to practise yoga only once in twenty-four hours unless specifically told to do so more often than that.

Place

Practise yoga on the floor. Avoid *chowki* or bed. Use a carpet, rug, blanket or mat on the floor. The place of practice should be neat, clean and well ventilated. There should be constant supply of fresh air at the place. Windows should be kept open for cross-ventilation. During summer a fan can be used. But during winter the draft of cold wind should be avoided. If the place is airconditioned, make sure that there is sufficient supply of air.

Silence

One should maintain silence while doing yoga. Any conversation, mental activity and even listening to music should be avoided. Silence helps in preserving energy as well as in being attentive during practice.

Rest

There are two types of rest in yoga: (i) short rest and (ii) long rest. The short rest should be for about six to eight seconds only. This is taken in between two rounds of the *asana*, or between one and the other *asana*. The shorter rest is completed by breathing twice at the completion of one round of a posture.

The long rest comes at the end of all the *asanas*, *pranayamas* and other *kriyas* which one does at a stretch. The general principle is to devote one fourth of the actual practising time for this rest. For example, if one has done yoga for twenty minutes, the rest at the end should be for five minutes.

The rest is better done in *Shava Asana*. Those who cannot do *Shava Asana* should just lie down on the floor, keeping the eyes closed, body loose, breathing normal, and concentrating the mind on any place of natural beauty such as a garden, park or hill side. In this simple method of resting there should be a feeling as if one is breathing the air of that chosen place and is relaxing by being mentally present there. After the rest is over, one should wait for three to five minutes before eating or doing any other routine work.

Dress

There should be minimum clothes on the body while doing yoga. Male practitioners can wear half-pants or *pyjamas* along with an underwear (such as, *langot or kachha*). Ladies can wear either sari, slacks or stretch-

17

pants with blouse. In winter, light woollen clothes may be used while doing yoga.

Bath

People generally want to know whether bath should be taken before or after yoga practice. For those practising yoga in the morning, it is not necessary to take a bath before they do it. It depends on the convenience and personal choice of the practitioner to bathe either before or after the practice. For taking a hot bath after yoga practise one must wait for about fifteen minutes. Many people prefer to practise yoga after taking a bath because there are certain *asanas* which are done better after the bath and it creates a feeling of neatness and purity.

Method of Practice

In order to obtain the fullest benefit of yoga, one must practise it in a proper way. Since yoga is a scientific system it requires to be done in a specified manner. If the *asanas*, *pranayamas*, *bandhas* and *mudras* are not done according to the established methods, it will become merely an exercise and will not give satisfactory results. The benefit of yoga on the body system is greater due to its methodology.[4]

What is more important here to mention is that though every one cannot practise all the postures with perfection, they can certainly follow the method of doing them without any difficulty. Therefore the advice is: do yoga according to the limits of your body. Do it only as much as you can. You need not be perfect in forms. If you cannot do the full form, do the half of it or even less[5].

---

[4]For understanding the scientific principles of yoga, see, Dr. Phulgenda Sinha, *Yoga: Meaning, Value and Practice* (Patna: Indian Institute of Yoga, 1970), pp. 2 to 8 or its paperback edition (Bombay:Jaico Publishing House, 1972) Chapter I.

[5]Such *asanas* whose final form cannot be performed with equal perfection by all, are mentioned with their variations in the text. In certain cases, the easier method and simple form of an *asana* is provided.

18

Follow all the steps carefully. Another important advice is to begin the practice with only a few *asanas* during the first week. When two or three *asanas* have been practised for a week, the next two *asanas* should be added during the second week. This way every week new *asanas* can be added according to the need and recommendation in a given case.

Female Problems

Female practitioners should avoid yoga practice during menstrual period and during advanced stage (after the fourth month) of pregnancy. Under such conditions, yoga practice should be generally discontinued. Yoga for pregnant women (after the fourth month) has to be performed on a selective basis under proper care and instruction of a yoga expert.

It is significant to mention that yoga has a great curative value for various ailments and disorders of women. It also works as an aid to their health. For example, menstrual disorders are corrected and normalized through yoga. Proper practice of yoga during early stages of pregnancy enhances the health of the child in womb and it also helps to make the delivery painless.

How Much Yoga

Yoga can be practised for a longer time in the winter season than in summer. Maximum time devoted for actually practising yoga should not exceed forty-five minutes in a single day of winter. In summer, the maximum time for actual practice should be thirty minutes. Time 'for rest may be allowed in addition according to the principle mentioned above. This difference in practising time has to be maintained because of variation in impact of weather on the body.

Though there should be only one session of yoga practice in a day, those who would like to divide their time in two sessions should allow a gap of eight hours between the first and the second session. A minimum practice of fifteen minutes per day should be quite satisfactory for maintaining good health.

With the above mentioned clarifications about therapeutic yoga and its basic requirements, let us now explain what is meant by 'Proper diet' in the yoga system. A proper understanding of some of the established principles and advice about diet would help the practitioners realise the importance of food and its impact on the body system in a better way. Though specific diet-charts are already mentioned for different types of diseases, the users of this book are advised to read the following section on 'proper diet' for a comprehensive knowledge of it.

Proper Diet

Diet occupies a dominant place in the yoga system. It is said that 'as you eat, so you become'. This is because the kind and quality of food affects the physical as well as mental condition of the individual. Thus, the individual who does not take a proper diet and who does not have a proper understanding of the principles of eating, gradually begins to harm himself both physically and mentally. He begins to feel the ill effects of wrong eating habits on his appearance, behaviour, thought and also on action. And the individual whose thought, action and appearance would not be desirable for a particular period of time would naturally show undesirable consequences which would justify the saying that 'as you eat, so you become'.

In yoga, all foods have been divided into three categories; *Rajasi, Tamasi* and *Sattvik*. These are explained below.

Rajasi

The *rajasi* food comprises a variety of dishes. It derives its name from the dining manners of Indian kings. It is said that no less than fifty-six dishes were served at a royal dining table. Naturally, in this type of preparations, dishes of various kinds—some fried, some roasted, and some curried and highly seasoned—together with various sweets and drinks would be served. Foods of this type are regarded undesirable for the yoga practitioners as they create extra weight and fat, generate feeling of heaviness for a longer period of time after dinner, and arouse passion.

Tamasi

The second category of eatables, that is the *tamasi* food include those which are prepared as hot stuffs. When any dish—vegetarian or non-vegetarian—is prepared with too many spices and with excessive uses of salts, pepper, chilli and similar other seasonings, it becomes *tamasi*. This type of food suits those who have a coarse nature and a rough temperament, and are inclined to be noisy, quarrelsome and intolerant. Hence, this type of food is undesirable and not recommended to the yoga practitioners.

Sattvik

In this type, the food is cooked with the least amount of spices and without much seasoning. The food is fresh, attractive and nutritive, and is cooked in a simple way. This type of food is desirable and highly recommended for the yoga practitioners.

According to yogic principles, no food whether vegetarian or non-vegetarian is by itself *rajasi, tamasi* or *sattvik*. What makes it this or that type is the method of preparation and not the food itself. The generally held notion that the non-vegetarian food is *tamasi* and the vegetarian food is *sattvik*, is wrong, because potato or cauliflower can be prepared as *tamasi* and meat or chicken can be cooked as *sattvik*, depending upon the choice of the individual.

The second point which needs clarification is that in yoga, food is not evaluated on the basis of their caloric count. Rather it is the quality of food and the method of eating that are considered. The better the quality of food, the more invigorating it is considered. Many people have a wrong notion that by reducing their intake of food or reducing the calories, they would lose extra weight. Similarly, many people feel that perhaps by eating heavily, they could gain weight. These notions are undesirable, as both these extremes have a harmful effect on the individual. Whether a person is overweight or underweight the yogic principles and methods of eating remain the same. One can gain or lose weight without any ill effects on his health by following the same yogic method of eating. What are then the yogic principles of eating?

Balanced Diet

The most important principle is to eat a balanced diet. When the following four things are included in everyday diet, the diet becomes balanced. These items are: salad, fresh vegetables, fresh fruits and raw nuts. To explain it further, whether you are a vegetarian or non-vegetarian, include these four items with your major dishes of the day.

Salad

All the vegetables that are eaten raw, constitute salad. Things such as cucumber, tomato, carrots, lettuce, cauliflower, etc., are used for preparing salad. These should be cut into pieces and with little dressing, can be eaten raw in the quantity of about a tea-cup per day. The ideal time to eat salad is to make it the first item of lunch and dinner.

Fresh Vegetables

Any vegetable which is not dried and is not deformed, can be regarded as fresh. They are to be preferred as fresh as possible. Fresh vegetables whether from under or above the ground, must be eaten in proportionate quantity everyday. They should, of course, be prepared in a *sattvik* way.

Fresh Fruits

Fruits constitute the most nutritive food for any individual. For better results from the Yogic practice, fresh fruits are essential. It is not necessary that one should take only the costly fruits, but any fruits that are easily available would serve the purpose. These fruits can be taken singly or mixed with various types. Fruits could be seasonal or year-round available types. How much to take? One apple, one orange, and one banana a day, for example, would be enough for an individual. The important point is that fruits should be eaten regularly for better health.

Raw Nuts

Nuts which are taken from hard shells are recommended. Such nuts are cashew, pistachio, almond, pecan and walnuts. A handful mixture of these nuts would be sufficient for a day. Since these raw nuts have a warm effect on the body, they should be taken in winter season and avoided or in less quantities in summer. Nuts from hard shells are full of proteins, minerals, and vitamins. Therefore, a proper intake of these nuts would be very energizing and healthy for yoga practitioners and non-practitioners alike.

Besides the above-mentioned items of balanced diet, there are some other principles of diet which must be followed for satisfactory results. They are:

Quantity of Food

Eat not more than about 85 per cent of your capacity. In other words, always keep some space left in your stomach after dinner. Do not overeat or even to your full capacity. When food is taken less than one's full capacity, it is easily digested and the body makes fuller use of the intakes. On the other hand, when the food is taken excessively and the stomach is completely stuffed, it is not properly digested and the body is forced to eliminate it without making proper use of it. Further, by eating more the individual is over-straining the abdominal system in particular and the body in general, and the performance of his physical and mental powers is obstructed. Gaining of extra and unnecessary weight is the natural outcome of overeating.

Method of Eating

The proper method is to eat slowly and swallow the food after thoroughly crushing and chewing it. One common error which the overweight people generally make is that they all eat too fast. It appears that the fast-eaters develop a habit and a taste wherein their satisfaction from food is only when they gollop it. To them, chewing and then swallowing is perhaps untasteful and boring. I recall a news item about a Texan(U.S.A.), whose dinner consisted of 18 chickens. He weighed more than 500 lbs., but he could not do much physical work. It can well be imagined that if he paid due attention to chewing all the chickens properly, he would be spending at least six to eight hours a day just for dinner, leave aside his breakfast, lunch and other refreshments. The repercussions of that type of eating have already been explained.

The yogic system, thus, takes into consideration the ill effects of fast eating and emphasises the importance of slow eating. But the question is: how slow? It depends on the type of food one is eating. For example, banana can be chewed faster than apple. Meat eating would take more time than fish. But in all circumstances, the guideline is to chew the food till it is rolled up and only then it should be swallowed.

There are may benefits of slow eating. The individual gets full satisfaction in dinner even when he eats only a small quantity of food. Saliva can be properly mixed up with the food and make it easily digestible. The body makes the full use of any food taken and the individual maintains better health by less amount of food.

Time Factor

Eat at least two hours before retiring time. A common error with most of the people is that they eat and then soon go to sleep, especially so during the night time. This has a very harmful effect upon their health. By keeping eating hours ahead of sleeping time, the food is properly processed by the body. The stomach is not heavy and when the individual goes to sleep, he gets undisturbed sleep and rest. Most of the people, who complain of abdominal, stomach or bowel troubles,are in the habit of eating and then immediately going to sleep. By so doing, they put undue strain on the abdominal muscles. They get disturbed sleep and most of the time they suffer from digestion ailments and disorders. Attention and care for early eating would correct these troubles.

Another important aspect which needs clarification is: how many times should one eat? It is rcommended that one should eat four times within a period of twenty-four hours. This means having breakfast in the morning, lunch at noon, some refreshment in the afternoon and dinner in the evening. It is up to the individual to eat according to his choice and preference, while keeping in mind the yogic principles. Unless one is faced with some special occasions, eating four times should be made a habit of daily life.

Spices

It is recommended not to use too much spices while preparing various dishes. This means not to use too much salt, chilli, pepper and other herbs. It is not to say that spices are bad. The objection is to excessive use of spices and seasoning. The seasoning can be done for flavour, but excessive use should be avoided. The food should be so seasoned that it does not become *tamasi*, but remains *sattvik* in nature.

Water

It is recommended that the yoga practitioners should drink about five lbs. (about ten to twelve glasses) of water every day. Water should not be taken at the time of eating, but after half an hour of eating. According to yogic literature, several skin diseases and disorders are corrected if water is not taken while eating. The drinking of plenty of water is highly recommended in yogic literature, because it is held that water cleans and washes out the impurities of the system. Many people do not drink enough water. I have personally known some people who were in the habit of drinking very little or not drinking water at all. Instead of water, they used to take juice, milk and some other liquids. As a result, they had developed a number of ailments and physical disorders. But most of these ailments were corrected when they started taking plenty of water every day. Therefore, the yoga practitioners should take five lbs. or more of fresh water within a period of twenty-four hours.

Coffee and Tea

Both coffee and tea are injurious to health when taken in excess. Modern people are now so much used to tea and coffee in their daily lives that it is not easy to abandon them. But a restraint on their intake must be maintained for better health. It is recommended that not more than two cups of tea or coffee should be taken in a period of twenty-four hours. There are various reasons for this restraint. Both these drinks if taken in large quantities, cause constipation, insomnia, nervous tension and other internal disorders. It has also been felt that an excess intake of these beverages distorts the natural complexion of the skin and also there is some roughening effect on the facial tissues. Therefore, a limit must be maintained in taking tea and coffee.

Alcoholic Drinks

All alcoholic drinks are regarded as vitamin thieves. They steal and destroy the nutrients of the system. Our objection to taking alcoholic drinks is not because they are intoxicative, but because they weaken the individual, physically and mentally, if taken without restraint. The destructive powers of alcoholic drinks are more in hard liquors and less in the weaker ones. But regardless of high or low alcoholic percentage in a drink, if a daily habit of drinking is maintained, it would prove extremely harmful. Therefore, the yoga practitioners are advised to avoid making it a habit of taking these drinks every day.

Gram (Chickpeas)

Sprouted gram is a very nutritious grain. It is full of protein, minerals and vitamins. Regular intake of a handful of germinated gram is highly conducive to good health. Yoga practitioners are, therefore, advised to make it a part of their daily eating. Green grams can be eaten fresh.

26

The ripe ones should be eaten after soaking in water for about eight hours. The sprouted grams are better than the plain ones, as the sprouted ones get enriched with energy derived from the air and light. It might be mentioned that if a person is not able to eat raw nuts and fruits regularly, he can compensate this loss by eating sprouted grams.

The recommendations on diet can be summed up by saying that yogic principles of diet are so simple that the yoga practitioners (whether vegetarian or non-vegetarian) should have no difficulty in following them. If these principles are followed closely and if the individual makes a habit of eating according to these recommendations, he is sure to maintain good health. A good balanced diet along with proper hygienic care, and a regular practice of yoga would guarantee developing and maintaining a proportionate figure and dynamic health.

Since enough has been said about proper diet and other requirements for yoga practitioners, we shall like to explain what is meant by hygienic care. Hygienic care includes proper bathing and cleaning habits. A discussion about the process of bathing and cleaning and their importance is provided in the following pages.

Bathing and Cleaning

Water is one of the three important things for survival of human beings. The other important items are air and food. Hence, a discussion about the value and uses of water is necessary. We know that several plants flourish on simply water and that some people can survive on water alone for several weeks and even months. This proves that in water there are life nourishing elements. This being the importance of water, the yoga practitioners must make a proper use of it by taking sufficient water.

Water can be used in two ways—internally and externally. In the preceding pages where we have recommended to drink at least five pounds of water within twenty-four hours the use is internal. Its external use is made through the process of washing and bathing.

In summer, one can bath twice daily. In winter and other seasons, bathing once a day is necessary for maintaining good health. One can use hot or cold water for bathing according to personal liking and the weather conditions.

It also needs to be explained how this external use of water benefits the individual. For this, we have to understand the structural and functional aspects of *romekoops*(pores).

The word *romekoop* is made of two Sanskrit words *rome* + *koop*. *Rome* means hair and *koop* means well. Thus its literal meaning would be a hair-well, which is called pore in English. We have millions of hair on our body and the root of each of them goes deeper in the body from the upper layer of the skin. At the root of every hair, there is a tiny hole which is not visible to the naked eye. These tiny holes at the roots of the hair are called *romekoops*. The body discards sweat and impurities of the system through these *romekoops* and allows penetration of air, water, etc., through them. Since these pores work as passages to and from the internal cells of the body for perspiration and absorption, the yogic system makes a greater and better use of them.

Hence, the primary consideration is how to make good use of the pores for benefitting the system. This is achieved by rubbing the whole body thoroughly while taking a bath, as it serves several purposes in a single process. But how to rub and clean?

Rubbing

There are several ways of rubbing the body during the bath, such as, with palms, washing cloth, sponge, brush or some other such thing. But the best thing to rub the body with, is the washing cloth or a small towel. The process is to get the washing cloth soaked in water, apply some soap on it and rub the whole body with it firmly while taking bath. Such rubbing serves several purposes. It opens the pores, excercises the upper layers of the skin, and makes it possible for the body to receive energy and life-nourishing elements by soaking water. This rubbing can be done with soap or without using soap. After rubbing the body, plenty of fresh water should be poured on the body.

Body Cleaning

Since we are talking about bathing, it is helpful to know something about soaps. In modern times, it is very difficult to think of bathing without using soap. Though we are not opposed to using soap, it must be understood that there are certain chemicals in it which do not suit the nature of skin of every individual. As we know, many people get rashes and rough skin after using certain types of soaps. Also, except cleaning the body, soaps do not contribute much to the good of the body. Thus, it is suggested that you must use a good quality soap, which is agreeable to your skin.

In the yogic system, the method of cleaning is different. There are several substitutes for soap. These substitutes not only clean the body but also contribute potentially to the health of the body. Amongst the yogic usables some are complicated and not easily available. Therefore, a simple but good material is recommended for this purpose.

One good substitute for soap is the gram (chick-peas) flour. Take a handful or more of gram flour and make a paste with lukewarm water in a pot. While going to take a bath, rub the whole body with this paste. Rub it with palms. After this rubbing, wash it with hot or cold water. Body will be cleaner than soap can clean it and will become smooth, soft and also invigorated with energy.

We have already said in the preceding pages that grams contain minerals, proteins and vitamins. Thus by using gram flour, the bather has two benefits at the same time— cleaning as well as invigorating the body. It can also be mentioned that gram flour cures many skin diseases and troubles such as itching, rough skin and similar other skin disorders.

Our recommendation is to use it at intervals of two to three days. This flour can also be used for cleaning the face and shampooing hair. Though for cleaning the face the process remains the same as for cleaning the body, for shampooing the hair some extra work is involved.

Shampooing

Take the kneaded flour and make a paste of it. Then put

it in thin cloth and tie it up. Now squeeze that paste containing cloth in water till the soft parts are mixed with water and only the rudiments remain in the cloth. When it has been well squeezed in water, throw the rudiments away and use that liquid type paste for shampooing hair. The squeezing of the paste is done to filter it in such a way that its rudiments are out and they do not get stuck with hair. The filtered paste will clean the hair of head in a very satisfactory and healthy way. Those who prefer to use other types of shampoos, should choose a really suitable kind for cleaning the hair. Hair should be shampooed once or twice a week.

Hair

Hair is the index of the health of the individual. Healthy hair generally means a healthy person. One simple way to keep the hair healthy is to rub at their roots at the time of taking a bath. The process is to pour some water on the head and rub with finger-tips at the roots of the hair till a warming-up effect is felt. After rubbing for a minute or so, pour plenty of water on the head. After the bath is over, dry the water from the head with clean and dry towel. Then after applying some hair oil or without using any oil, comb the hair. Comb the hair twice or thrice a day by giving a pull to the opposite, i.e. from top down, down up, left to right and right to left. By this combing process, the hair would be stronger and would be prevented from falling.

Some people have a false notion that by rubbing and combing, they would lose their hair. Though the person who has dandruff might lose some hair by rubbing and combing in the initial stage, the falling of the hair would stop after a week or so. Moreover, new hair would soon begin to grow. This rubbing and combing method is equally good for men and women.

Teeth

Like hair, teeth also symbolize the health of an individual. The simple way of keeping the teeth healthy is to brush them and massage the roots. Besides the morning cleaning, teeth must be brushed before retiring at night.

The brushing should be done in upward and downward motions and not sideways. The next thing is to rub the root of the teeth. This is done by taking some paste on the fingers and putting the thumb inside and the index finger outside and then rubbing the gums firmly. It is sufficient to rub the gums with paste or tooth-powder once in twenty-four hours. This makes the gums grow stronger and stops decay.

Oil Massage

Among various oils used for massaging, mustard oil is the best. Mustard oil is commonly used in India for cooking, applying to the hair, etc. It is also used for massaging the babies as well as by wrestlers and old people. It is a healthy and invigorating oil. Since it has a warm effect on the body, the yoga practitioners are advised to apply it only during the winter season, not during summer. When it is applied to the body, it penetrates through the pores and imparts elasticity and strength to the muscles, bones and nerves. It soothes, cleans, gives a good, tanned complexion to the body and makes the skin healthy. It also helps to remove the wrinkles and dryness of the skin.

How to use it? Take some oil on the palms and smear it on parts of the body and give light rubbing till it is partially soaked. Apply it all over the body and leave it there for ten to fifteen minutes. In that time, part of the oil will be soaked by the body through the pores.

You can clean the oil from the body in two ways. First take a shower without using soap and rub the body using either warm or cold water, then wipe out the oily remnants from the body with a dry and clean towel. As the oil is wiped off, the body would gain a clean and smooth look.

The second process is that after smearing oil, use gram-flour paste as a substitute for soap. Apply that paste all over the oily body and rub it with palms till the paste is fully mixed up with oil. After the rubbing wash it off with either cold or hot water. Gram flour paste will clean the oil in a more thorough and satisfactory way than soap can do

31

it. By so doing, you have the benefit of both oil and flour. This can be regarded as a beautifying treatment, as it enhances the natural look of the skin.

This application of oil and cleaning with the paste should be done on alternate days, or once or twice a week but not every day. If someone prefers to use soap in between the application of oil and paste, there is nothing objectionable. In case soap is used, the choice should be made in such a way that it is nature and the condition of the skin of the users.

Let me sum up this chapter by saying that all the basic information and suggestions regarding therapeutic yoga have been carefully mentioned in the foregoing pages. You are advised to read this whole chapter carefully so that you develop a proper understanding of the yogic system of treatment and then start the actual practice. Remember that you are following 'a system of self-treatment' without relying on or using medicine. Therefore, it is important that you understand it first for satisfactory results. Keeping in mind the contents of this chapter, select the section of your concern and begin the practice of yoga according to the guidelines given therein.

2

Abdominal Disorders

ALL SUCH troubles that disturb the normal functioning of the digestive system have been termed here as abdominal disorders. The commonly found disorders in this case are: constipation, wind formation, indigestion, dysentery, diarrhoea, acidity, stomach ache and various forms of gastrointestinal disorders. Our experience shows that it is a widely prevalent problem of our times, affecting young and old alike.

Though the causes of abdominal disorders could be varied and multiple, the most common are: (i) the psychosomatic factors, such as nervousness, tension and various forms of stress and strain; and (ii) improper eating habits, such as over-eating, eating at irregular hours, going to bed immediately after the evening meals, not eating a balanced diet, excessive use of hot spices and fried things, eating adulterated and stale food stuffs, not chewing the food properly, unhygienic ways of eating, etc.

We have found that these disorders are easily curable through the yogic system of treatment. In most cases, the trouble is controlled within two weeks and it is fully cured in about two months. Let us explain how people suffering from these troubles can cure themselves by following the yoga system of practice.

The yoga system of treatment requires: (i) daily practice of a few *asanas* and (ii) proper diet.

Yogic Treatment

The important *pranayama* and *asanas* for correcting these disorders are: *Pranayama* with *Rechaka* and *Puraka, Uttanpada Asana, Pawanmukta Asana, Bhujanga Asana, Shalabha Asana, Paschimottan Asana,* and *Shava Asana.* The method of practising these asanas and the pranayama are comprehensively described and illustrated in the following pages:

PRANAYAMA (with Rechaka and Puraka)

Pranayama is a special form of breathing exercise. There are various forms of *pranayama*. Though each form is done differently, most of them have the following three steps in common:

Rechaka (Exhalation)
Puraka (Inhalation)
Kumbhaka(Retention)

In this particular *pranayama*, there are only *rechaka* and *puraka* but no *kumbhaka* (retention of the breath). One significant aspect of this *pranayama* is that it is a diaphragmatic breathing. In this exercise the stomach is pulled in and forward in a rhythmic way. It is very important to remember that the stomach is not pushed upward and downward.

Position of Readiness

Sit down on the floor either in *Padma Asana* (Lotus pose) as shown in Fig. 1,* or in *Sukha Asana* (Easy pose) as

---

*The figure numbers here and elsewhere in the book refer to the appropriate pictures, all of which are numbered, for example Fig. 1 means picture No. 1 given on page 49 and so on.

shown in Fig. 2. Hold the spine, neck and head absolutely erect. Look forward, straight at the level of your eyes. Stretch your arms and rest your wrists on the knees. Bring your thumb and index finger of each hand to meet together so that they form a circle and keep the other three fingers opened straight and joined together. Breathe normally.

Steps for Practice

(i) Exhale slowly through both nostrils and simultaneously pull your stomach inwards, i.e. contract the abdominal muscles to expel air from your lungs. Keep exhaling till all the air is expelled.

(ii) Having exhaled, hold yourself in that position for a second and then slowly start inhaling through both nostrils. Inhale as deeply as you can by stretching out the abdominal muscles. The expansion of the stomach with inhalation should be gradual and rhythmical, not abrupt and fast.

(iii) After inhaling deeply, pause for a second and then start exhaling again. Continue this process for ten to fifteen times, (one exhalation and one inhalation each time).

Daily Practice

During the first week of practice, do this excercise ten times daily. During the second week and afterwards, increase it to fifteen times. But do not do it more than fifteen times in a single day.

Special Attention

As long as this *pranayama* continues, it is essential to keep the spine straight. The head, the neck and the spine should remain in a straight line all along the exercise. After the exercise is over every day, hold yourself in the same position for a few seconds, and breathe normally. Then gradually relax into a more comfortable position. Do other *asanas* after waiting for five to ten seconds.

Benefits

It activates all the organs of the digestive system. Because of this internal activation, disorders of the digestive system are removed and corrected. Problems like constipation, dysentery, diarrhoea, gastric indigestion, and stomach ache are corrected.

This *pranayama* also effects various glands of the endocrine system. The adrenal, pancreas, ovary in female and testicles in male are specially activated and energized. Because of their internal activation, these glands begin to secrete their respective hormones in a normal way.

It also corrects disorders of the circulatory and respiratory systems. It is an easy *pranayama* and can be practised by any person without any difficulty.

UTTANPADA ASANA

Position of Readiness

Lie with your back on the floor and look upwards at the ceiling. Keep both the arms straight alongside the body with palms touching the floor. Straighten both the legs and join your heels and toes. Breathe normally.

Steps for Practice

(i) Inhale slowly but deeply through both nostrils and hold the breath.

(ii) Stretch out both your toes as much as you can.

(iii) While holding the breath slowly lift both legs up, about ten to twelve inches high from the floor and keep them there for six to eight seconds as shown in Fig. 3.

(iv) Then start exhaling and lowering the legs towards the floor, both acts so synchronized that the legs reach the floor as you finish exhaling.

(v) Now rest for two normal breaths which should take about five to six seconds.

(vi) After resting, repeat the process.

Daily Practice

Do it four times daily. Do not practise more than five times in a single day.

Note: Those who have suffered any back injury or are otherwise weak, should not do this *asana* with both legs. They are advised to practise *Uttanpada Asana* with only one leg at a time (as shown in Fig. 4), till they get used to its impact. After practising with one leg at a time for about four weeks, they may start with both legs together.

The reason for this precaution is that *Uttanpada Asana* brings great strain on the whole of spine and also on the rest of the body. This strain is cut to half by doing the *asana* with one leg only. The process of doing with one leg is the same as for doing with both legs. The only difference is that instead of lifting both legs together at a time, you have to lift only one leg and leave the other on the floor. Do it alternately, with the other leg, completing three times with each leg. Do not practise for more than six times at a stretch.

Benefits

This *asana* exercises all the abdominal muscles, both internally and externally. As a result, this *asana* corrects disorders of the pancreas and cures constipation, wind troubles, indigestion and intestinal disorders. It takes away the extra weight of the abdominal area.

This *asana* also has great curative and corrective effect on backache or troubles in the waist, buttocks and hip-joints. It strengthens the spinal cord, energizes the inner cells and activates the whole nervous system.

PAWANMUKTA ASANA

Position of Readiness

Stand up on the floor. Keep both hands hanging down. Look straight on the same level as is the height of your eyes from the floor.

Steps for Practice

(i) Lift one knee up towards the chest.

(ii) Put the same side hand on the ankle and the other hand on the knee as shown in Fig. 5.

(iii) Pull the knee towards the chest without any pull on the ankle.

(iv) Stand firmly on the other leg, keeping quite straight.

(v) Stay in that position for six to eight seconds; then release the knee and put the foot on the floor.

(vi) Rest for six seconds and repeat the same process with the other leg.

Daily Practice

Do it six to eight times daily (three to four times with each knee alternately).

Note: Those who feel difficulty in performing this *asana* in the standing position, may do it lying on the back. Method of practice remains the same as in the standing position. There is also an advantage of flexibility of limbs as one performs this *asana* in lying position.

Benefits

It activates the pancreas and other organs of the abdomen in a mild and effective way. It is also a wind reliever. For people suffering from wind trouble, acidity and gas formation, it has an instant corrective effect. It loosens the hip-joints and activates the whole of abdominal muscles and intestines. As a result of its internal activation, it cures constipation, and corrects any malfunctioning of the stomach. Because of these internal impacts it helps to restore the functioning of the pancreas. It is an easy and harmless *asana*. Any person can do it.

BHUJANGA ASANA

Position of Readiness

Lie on the stomach. Let the head rest on any cheek. Bring the palms beneath the shoulders on both sides. Let the tips of fingers be at the edge of shoulders. Elbows should be folded upward closer to the body. Keep the heels together and the toes flat on the floor. Breathe normally.

Steps for Practice

(i) Straighten the head and tilt it slightly backward.

(ii) Inhaling slowly, raise your head and chest upwards so that while your navel is on the floor, the portion above the navel is raised up. In this position your both legs should be fully stretched and kept tightly together as shown in Fig. 6.

(iii) Then look up into the sky and hold your breath for six to eight seconds.

(iv) After six to eight seconds, start exhaling and lowering the head towards the floor and let the head rest on any cheek.

(v) Now let the body relax and rest for six seconds.

(vi) After rest, repeat the process.

Daily Practice

Repeat it only four times daily

Benefits

Bhujanga Asana inwardly activates the whole of abdominal area. Because of this activation, the pancreas, liver and other organs of the digestive system are strengthened and normalized. It is regarded as one of the best *asanas* for curing constipation, indigestion, dysentery, wind troubles, stomach ache and other abdominal disorders. It brings flexibility to the spine and corrects spinal disorders and backache. It activates chest, shoulders, neck, face and head areas in an effective way and enhances facial beauty. Various menstrual problems are corrected by this *asana*.

SHALABHA ASANA

Position of Readiness

Lie down on your stomach. Put any cheek on the floor. Stretch the hands on both sides of the body and keep them close to the thighs. Keep the thumb and index finger side of the palms down on the floor and make fists with both hands in the same position. Stretch both the legs and let the toes be flat down on the floor. Keep the heels together and toes together. Keep the whole body straight. Breathe normally. Now you are ready for making the *asana*.

Steps for Practice

(i) Inhale slowly but deeply through both nostrils and hold the breath.

(ii) Lift the head slightly, make it straight and then let the chin rest on the floor (use a folded towel underneath the chin).

(iii) Make the fists firm and tighten the arms and the hands.

(iv) Now tighten both the legs together and lift them up quickly as high as you easily can.

(v) Stay in that position for five to six seconds or less, keeping the legs quite tight all over (as shown in Fig. 7).

(vi) Then exhale slowly, simultaneously lowering the legs down towards the floor.

(vii) When the legs have touched the floor, turn the head to let it rest on the either cheek; and let the whole body loose.

(viii) Rest for five seconds; then repeat the *asana* in the same order as before.

Daily Practice

Repeat it only four times daily. (Do it after performing the *Bhujanga Asana*).

Note: Those who might feel difficulty in lifting both legs together are advised to lift only one leg at a time (as shown in Fig. 8) for a few weeks. In this case, practise six rounds alternately three times with each leg. Later on one can practise this *asana* with both legs.

Benefits

It has curative effect on various abdominal troubles. It activates the kidneys, the liver, pancreas, and the whole of abdominal area. Because of internal activation, it removes constipation, wind troubles, indigestion, dysentery, diarrhoea, acidity and gastro-intestinal disorders.

This *asana* has also various other good effects on the body as a whole. It brings flexibility to the spine and invigorates the eyes, the face, lungs, chest, neck, shoulders and the whole upper area of the body. Since it is a harmless *asana*, it is recommended for every practitioner.

PASHCHIMOTTAN ASANA

Position of Readiness

Sit on the floor and stretch both your legs in front. Keep the heels and toes together. Be seated firmly, keeping the spine, neck and head straight upward. At this stage, keep the hands down on the floor on both sides.

Steps for Practice

(i) Stretch out both the arms parallel to the stretched legs.

(ii) Touch the right toe with the right hand fingers and the left toe with the left hand fingers (as shown in Fig. 9). In case you cannot touch the toes, go only as far as possible while keeping both the legs stretched and palms down. Do not fold or lift the toes.

(iii) Bow your head downwards till it comes between the two arms. Exhale all the air out by the time head is down.

(iv) Now stretch the toes and tighten the legs, and while keeping the head between the two arms, stretch both hands as much forward as possible. Without bending the legs at the knees, stay in that position for six to eight seconds (as show in Fig. 10).

(v) Now drop both palms on the legs and start inhaling and returning to the position of readiness. Let the palms be dragged back over the legs while returning.

(vi) Rest for five seconds and repeat the process.

Daily Practice

Do it four times daily. (Practise at least three times and at most five times a day.)

41

Note: Those who had back injury or spinal disorders with severe pain are advised to practise lightly and comfortably without forcing the body to bend excessively. Care should be taken not to stretch the muscles abruptly.

Benefits

This *asana* has effect on the whole of the spinal cord, the complete nervous system and all the organs and glands of the abdominal area. As a result of these activations, disorders of these parts are corrected. For the diabetic people it has a curative effect because it activates the pancreas and the glands of the endocrinal system. This internal activation regularizes the functioning of the pancreas and it begins to secrete insulin in a normal way.

This *asana* gives several other good results. It corrects backache, cures spinal disorders, relieves stomach troubles, and normalizes the functioning of the nervous system.

For many people, it might not be possible to do this *asana* accurately. They are advised to do only as much as they can comfortably do. In due course, after practising for a while, they will improve and will begin to do satisfactorily. Remember that the method of doing an *asana* is important than repeating it for a number of times. Since it is a very beneficial *asana*, it is recommended to every practitioner.

SHAVA ASANA

Position of Readiness

Lie down on your back. Keep the whole body loose and in a straight position. Palms can be either on the floor or you can keep them upwardly. Do not use any pillow under your head. At this point keep breathing in normal way. Keep the eyes closed and let the whole body fall on the floor in an unrestrained way. This is the position of readiness and the same position remains during the actual practice (see fig.11)

Steps for Practice

(i) Close your eyes and keep them closed for two seconds. Then open them for two seconds. Do this simple opening and closing of the eyes for three to four times.

(ii) Open the eyes again and look upward, then downward, then straight. Now look towards the left side, then towards the right side, then straight again and then close the eyes. Repeat this eye exercise two to three times.

(iii) Now open your mouth wide without straining it. Turn the tongue inside the mouth in such a way that its tip is folded back towards the throat area, then close the mouth. Keep the mouth closed and tongue folded for 10 seconds. Then open the mouth and bring the tongue back to its normal position, then close the mouth. Repeat the process for two to three rounds.

(iv) Keeping your eyes closed, bring your mental attention towards your toes. See (mentally) that the toes are relaxed. Then move slowly upward and towards the head area mentally by checking the knees, thighs, waist, spinal cord, back, shoulders, neck, arms, palms, fingers and rest of the areas of the body to be sure that they are actually relaxed. Make a slight movement of the neck and head by turning right and left. Then let the head rest at a comfortable position. Now the entire body is physically relaxed.

(v) Then relax the mind with the following process:

Select a place of natural beauty which you have ever visited and liked, such as, a park, a garden, a lawn or a riverside and feel as if you are mentally present at that place. Attach your mind to that place. Feel as if you are lying at that place and breathing the air of the same environment. Now while keeping the mind involved with that environment, do some deep breathing. In this deep breathing, just exhale and inhale slowly but deeply. During the breathing, the stomach should go upward while inhaling and it should come downward while exhaling. One exhalation and one inhalation make one round. Do not rush in this deep breathing. Make about ten to twelve rounds. When the deep breathing is over, feel as if you are going to sleep. Now relax completely. Stay in that position for five to ten minutes. Then open your eyes and stretch your body and then be seated. You have completed the *Shavasana*.

Daily Practice

Make *Shavasana* at the end of all *asanas, pranayama* and other *kriyas* for 10-15 minutes daily. In certain cases like hypertension and heart troubles, *Shavasana* should be performed singly for longer periods without practising any *asana* or other *kriyas*.

Benefits

Shavasana has a very good effect upon the patients as well as upon any yoga practitioner. One immediate effect is that it relaxes all the muscles, nerves and the organs of the body system. When the muscles, nerves and organs are fully relaxed, they gain strength and their normal health is restored.

For the people suffering from insomnia, high and low blood pressure, gastric troubles, lungs and heart troubles and mental sickness, *Shavasana* is a remarkable *kriya* for providing immediate relief. Those who feel lack of energy, tiredness, fatigue and lack of vitality will find this *asana* as a giver of energy and strength. Because of these good effects, every practitioner of yoga is advised to practise it.

Proper Diet

Eat a balanced diet which should include salad, green vegetables and fresh fruits along with other dishes of the day. Eat at least two hours before going to bed at night. Eat not more than about eight five percent of your capacity. Do not drink water during meals, but only about after half an hour of finishing your meals. Take ten to twelve glasses of water every day. Avoid fried, roasted and spicy food. Exclude red pepper, pickles, hot spices, *chutney* and *arhar dal* from your menu. Do not take more than two cups of tea or coffee in a day. If possible stop taking tea and coffe at all for a while. Also, do not take coke and other aerated drinks. Must stop bed-tea or drinking of water as you get

44

up in the morning. Non-vegetarians can take fish or liver but should avoid meat for a while. People with any kind of abdominal disorder should eat according to the diet chart given below:

Breakfast (7 to 9 A.M.)

(i)	Orange juice or any fruit juice	- One cup
	or sweet orange or *mausami*	- One
(ii)	Fresh apple or any fresh fruit	- One
	(except mangoes and lichi)	
(iii)	Germinated gram	- 1/4 cup
(iv)	Wheat bread with green vegetable/or wheat *dalia*/oat-meal/corn flakes, milk and sugar	
(v)	Cheese	-One slice
(vi)	Egg (poached, boiled or scrambled)	-One
(vii)	Tea, coffee or ovaltine	-One cup

Lunch (12 to 2 P.M.)

(i)	Salad (a mixture of tomato, cucumber, radish, lettuce, carrot, etc., with salt, pepper and lemon juice or salad dressing)	- About a cup
(ii)	Vegetable soup	- One cup
(iii)	Rice or wheat bread *(chapati)*	
(iv)	Pulse *(moong, masur or chana)*	
(v)	*Saag* (green leaves of any variety)	
(vi)	Green vegetables (fresh vegetables of any kind)	

Afternoon Refreshments (3 to 5 P.M.)

(i)	Fresh fruit of any type	
(ii)	Salted biscuits or any light food (easily digestible)	
(iii)	Cheese	- One slice
(iv)	Tea, coffee or ovaltine	- One cup

Dinner (7 to 9 P.M.)

(i)	Salad	- One cup
(ii)	Vegetable soup	- One cup

(iii) Wheat bread (*chapati*)

(iv) Pulse (*moong, masur, urad or chana*)

(v) *Saag* (green leaves of any variety)

(vi) Green vegetables (fresh vegetables of any kind)

(vii) Fish or liver.

3

Diabetes

THIS CHAPTER presents the process of curing diabetes through yoga. We know that diabetes is a very old disease and millions all over the world suffer from it. Though there are variations in the symptoms and nature of this disease, its common feature is the excessive sugar in the blood and its passing out with the urine of the patients. This excessive accumulation of sugar in the blood is caused by the malfunctioning of the pancreas.

When the pancreas—a gland situated in the upper side of abdomen—does not produce enough insulin, the body fails to utilize the sugar and create energy from it. In the absence of proper utilization of sugar, the body chemistry gets disturbed and the individual begins to develop various physical ailments and disorders. Consequently, there is frequent urination, excessive tiredness, loss of weight, blurring of the vision, general weakness and skin disorders in diabetic patients. Further with chronicity, hypertension (high blood pressure) and kidney disorders also develop. The general prevalent method of treating the diabetic patient is to inject insulin to compensate what could not be produced by the pancreas.

The main trouble with medicinal treatment is that the patient has to keep taking injections and other medicines indefinitely and still the disease is not eliminated.

Yogic Treatment

The yogic system of treatment consists of two aspects: (i) proper diet, and (ii) regular yoga practice. In the initial stage, the patient can start yoga practice without stopping the medicine or injections, if he happens to be under medical treatment. After practising yoga for about three weeks, the person should gradually reduce and finally stop taking the medicines.

While treating the diabetic patients at the Indian Institute of Yoga, we have found that it takes from two to three months to cure this disease.[1]

The yogic treatment restores the normal functioning of the pancreas and other glands of the endocrinal system. When these glands begin to function properly, the body chemistry becomes normal, the individual is fully cured of the diabetic disorders and his health is restored to normal level.

Relevant Asanas

Since the main problem here is to restore the normal functioning of the pancreas and some other glands, the first consideration is to select such *asanas* which can help to revive the normal functioning of the endocrinal system. Secondly, we should choose such *asanas* which are easier to be practised by all. Accordingly, the *asanas* we may recommend are: *Surya Namaskar Asana, Uttanpada Asana, Bhujanga Asana, Shalabha Asana, Paschimottan Asana, Ardha Vakra Asana, Matsyendra Asana, Supta*

[1] We have found that diabetes among people over forty years of age is cured sooner than among people below forty. The juvenile diabetes (below twenty years of age) may take about a year or more for complete cure.

Fig 1   Padma Asana

Fig 2   Sukha Asana

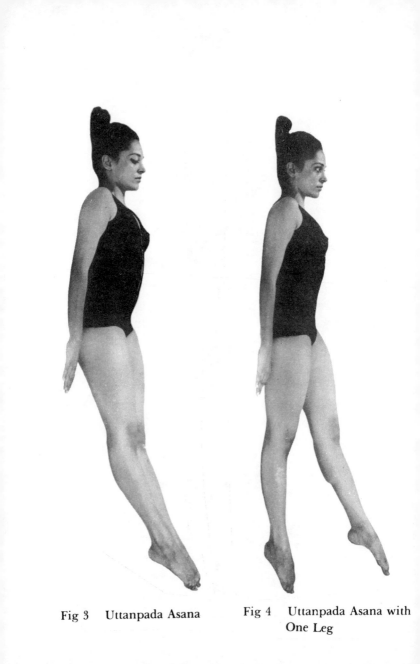

Fig 3   Uttanpada Asana

Fig 4   Uttanpada Asana with One Leg

Fig 5   Pawanmukta Asana

Fig 6   Bhujanga Asana

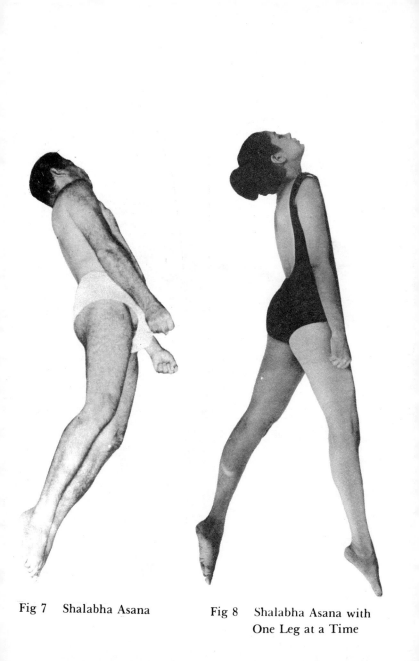

Fig 7   Shalabha Asana

Fig 8   Shalabha Asana with
One Leg at a Time

Fig 9   Readiness for Pashchimottan Asana

Vajra Asana, Dhanur Asana and *Shava Asana*. A regular practise of even six to seven of these *asanas* would be enough to cure diabetes.

SURYANAMASKAR ASANA

Position of Readiness

Stand up keeping the legs apart at about two feet distance. Let the hands hang loosely at your sides. Keep the head straight. Look directly in front and breathe normally.

Steps for Practice

(i) Inhale slowly and raise both hands towards the sky, in sidewise circular movement. Time it in such a way that by the time your hands come up, you also complete inhaling. When the hands are up, the palms should be turned forward and the arms should be in a parallel position.

(ii) Start exhaling and lowering the upper area of the body towards the ground. While thus bending forward, keep both hands parallel to one another and move them towards the ground, in a circular motion in front of you. By the time both hands reach near the floor, you should finish exhaling.

(iii) Now hold the breath and stay in that position for about six to eight seconds. While holding your breath, it is important that you keep the upper part of the body (above the waist) quite loose, and the lower part, i.e., the waist and the lower part, rigid and hard. Bend your head down towards the ground. Your head should be between the two arms. Hands should be loosely hanging as far down as they can easily go. If you can bend easily, put the palms on the floor or just touch the floor. It is important that you are not straining yourself or forcing your body excessively for making the bend. Do only as much as you can do very comfortably (see Fig. 12).

(iv) Bring both hands on the legs and inhale and come

up in the standing position. While coming up let the palms pass over and touch the legs upward. Inhale slowly in such a way that by the time you have returned to the standing position you have finished inhaling. Now you have completed one round of *Suryanamaskar Asana*.

(v) Rest for five to six seconds and then repeat the same process. Stay in the position of readiness while resting.

Daily Practice

Practise four times daily. Do not do it more than four times in a single day.

Benefits

This *asana* has several benefits. It activates almost all the glands of the endocrinal system in a mild way. Because of this internal activation, the pancreas, adrenal, thyroid, pituitary and some other glands begin to secrete their respective hormones in a normal way. Since the main trouble with persons of diabetic disorder results from the malfunctioning of the pancreas, this *asana* corrects its defects by activating it.

It has good effect on the stomach, spine, lungs and chest. Various disorders of these areas are corrected by this *asana*. As there is reverse circulation of blood during this *asana*, it invigorates the facial tissues, the central nervous system and all the organs of the upper part of the body. It is easy to do and therefore recommended to all practitioners of yoga.

After practising *Suryanamaskar Asana*, the following *asanas* should be gradually added to daily practice.

Uttanpada Asana	(See Fig. 3 and 4)
Bhujanga Asana	(See Fig. 6)
Shalabha Asana	(See Fig. 7 and 8)
Paschimottan Asana	(See Fig. 9 and 10)

These four *asanas* are fully described in chapter 2 (under the heading "Abdominal Disorders"). The diabetic patients are advised to practise these *asanas* according to the method described therein.

ARDHAVAKRA ASANA

Position of Readiness

Sit down on the floor. Stretch both legs in front. Make the legs parallel to one another. Put both palms on the floor. Breathe normally. Keep the back straight while sitting.

Steps for Practice

(i) Let one leg remain stretched on the floor. Fold the other leg at the knee and pull it slightly backward.

(ii) Put the heel of the folded leg at the central point between the knee and the ankle of the stretched leg. Then drop the heel on the outer side of the leg. Keep the heel quite close to the stretched leg. Now the knee of your folded leg should be upward.

(iii) Lift the hand which is on the side of the stretched leg; bring it up and parallel to the stretched leg. Grab the stretched leg near the heel of the folded leg. Now you have made a lock with the arm and the knee. If you cannot grab the stretched leg, just touch it or keep the fingers near the central point.

(iv) Lift the other side hand and put its palm on the waist, keeping the thumb and the index finger side upward. Now your elbow is folded and making a 90 degrees angle with the stretched leg. At this stage see that your head, neck and back are straight upward.

(v) Start exhaling slowly and at the same time begin twisting and turning the waist, chest, neck and the head area in the direction of the folded elbow. Twist and turn as much as you comfortably can. In this turn, your folded elbow travels 90 degrees but the head and the upper area of the body travel 180 degrees. For example, if you were sitting facing east and you have to turn right then your face will turn first to south and then to the west while your stretched leg will remain facing east.

(vi) After making the maximum turn, hold the breath and stay in that position for six to eight seconds. At this stage, your spine should be straight upwards and you should be projecting the vision at a maximum distance (as shown in Fig. 13).

(vii) Then start inhaling slowly and return to the position of readiness.

(viii) Now break the lock, stretch out the legs, relax the body, put the palms on the floor and rest for six seconds.

(ix) After rest repeat the *asana* with the other leg, following the same method.

Daily Practice

Make four to six rounds alternately. Never do it more than six times (three times with each side).

Benefits

The main effect of this *asana* is on the waist and abdominal areas. It activizes all the organs and glands of these parts of the body. This *asana* has a very good effect on the pancreas, adrenal, ovary in female and the testicles in male.

It has several other good benefits. It corrects constipation, stomach troubles, piles, backache, stiffness in the neck and spinal disorders. It is easy to do and therefore recommended to every practitioner of yoga.

MATSYENDRA ASANA

Matsyendra Asana is a little difficult. It may not be possible for everyone to do it perfectly in the beginning. But since it is an important *asana*, the practioners are advised to do it as much as they can do comfortably. People who can practise *Matsyendra Asana* perfectly should not practise *Ardhavakra Asana* as both have similar effect. Since *Ardhavakra Asana* is easier to do, the practitioners should begin with it.

Position of Readiness

Be seated on the floor. Stretch both legs in front. Keep the legs in a parallel position. Put the palms on the floor on both sides of the body. Straighten the body. Look in front and breathe normally.

Steps for Practice

(i) Fold the right leg at the knee by pulling it backward. Now the right thigh is standing upward and the right side buttock has been raised up. At this stage, keep this right leg where it is standing.

(ii) Fold the left leg at the knee without lifting it up. The thigh and knee of the left leg should remain on the floor and the foot should be brought below the right buttock. The left foot may be gently pulled by hand for bringing it underneath the buttock.

(iii) Now lift the right foot slightly up and bring it on the outer side of the folded left knee. Keep the right foot quite close to the folded left knee. Now your right knee is standing upward and the left knee is down on the floor.

(iv) Then you have to make a lock with the opposite arm and the standing knee. Since your right knee is standing, you have to make the lock with the left arm, therefore, stretch out the left arm and bring it on the outer side of the right knee. Now your arm is locked against the standing knee firmly. Grab the right foot with the left hand in order to provide stability to the locked part of the body.

(v) Bring the whole of right arm and hand on the back in a loose condition. Try to touch the front part of the fingers of hand on the back. You are now ready for making the turn. At this stage see that your backbone, neck and head are in a straight upward position.

(vi) Now start exhaling slowly and turning the head, chest and waist areas towards the right side. Twist the body as much as you can. Be sure that all air has been thrown out by the time you have made the full twist. Look at the farthest distance outside. Keep the back straight upward. You should be as in Fig. 14.

(vii) Stay in that position for six to eight seconds. The holding time may be for only four to six seconds in the beginning of practice.

(viii) Then start inhaling slowly and gradually return to

the position from 'where you had started the twist. You have completed one round of *Matsyendra Asana*.

(ix) Now unlock the arm, the knee and be seated in the position of readines and rest for six to eight seconds. During the rest just inhale and exhale deeply two times.

(x) After the rest make preparation for turning to the left side in another round. Now your left knee will be standing up and your right arm will be locked. You have to keep doing it alternatively.

Daily Practice

Make four to six rounds daily. Do not ever practice it more than six rounds. Do it alternately and only as much as is possible without undue strain.

Benefits

This *asana* has great effect on the pancreas and other glands, such as, adrenal, thyroid and the sex glands. The muscle and organs of the abdominal area are fully activated due to this *asana*. Because of this activation the condition and functioning of the pancreas is energized and strengthened. This is the reason that people suffering from diabetes are advised to practise this *asana* daily even if they cannot do it quite properly.

This *asana* has several other benefits for any practitioner of yoga. It corrects disorders of kidneys, spleen, liver, stomach, intestine, bladder and the pelvic region because of their internal activation by this *asana*.

This has also good effect on lungs because of improvement in blood circulation by this *asana*. People with breathlessness are advised to begin this *asana* in a mild way and gradually develop it to perfection.

This *asana* has some specific benefits in cases of spinal disorders. It removes rigidity of the spine and restores flexibility in it. Since it twists the whole of spinal cord from cervical to the coccyx in an effective and mild way the disorders of the whole spine are corrected.

Since it is a very beneficial *asana* for the diabetic people as well as for others, all practitioners are advised to do it.

SUPTAVAJRA ASANA

Position of Readiness

Sit on the floor with your legs folded under you. See Fig. 15. Put the palms on the floor on both sides of the body and straighten your spine. Now look in front and breathe normally.

Note: This *asana* is a little difficult. Those whose body condition is not very flexible are advised to practise this *asana* in a gradual way without trying to do the complete *asana* all at once. It can be done without any strain in stages, and soon one can perform it with easiness.

Steps for Practice

(i)   Kneel on the floor, keeping the body weight on both the knees. Put the palms on the floor on both sides of the folded knees to support part of the body weight. Keep the knees about four inches apart from one another. Let the ankles and toes of both the legs fall on the floor in such a way that the toes are brought close together but the heels are spread out. This will make a broad "V" curve with the toes, soles and the heels.

(ii) Now gradually and cautiously start lowering the hip and let it rest on the curve of the soles. Control the body weight by keeping both hands on the floor while lowering the hip. If you do not feel strained, put the whole body weight on the curve of the feet as shown in Fig. 15. In case of difficulty in sitting in this position, further stages should not be tried till the body is prepared for it. Those who can sit comfortably on the toes and soles should proceed to the third stage.

(iii) Lift the right hand and place it on the floor behind the hips. Then move the left hand also behind the hip and bend a little backward.

(iv) Now put the right elbow on the floor by bending backward. Then put the left elbow on the floor. By moving the elbows towards the hip gradually let the head touch the floor. When the head has come down on the ground,

63

gradually put the shoulder and then the whole back of your body on the floor. Do not rush. Go slow in this process.

(v) Now you stretch both the arms and hands on both sides of the body. Keep the palms on the floor and close to the body, as shown in Fig. 16.

(vi) Then do a few deep breathing exercises by just inhaling and exhaling the air through both nostrils.Stay in that position for six to eight seconds or less. You are in *Suptavajra Asana.*

(vii) Now you have to return with the following method: Grab the ankles with the hands and put the elbows on the floor. Now pull the ankles and by putting the weight of the body on the elbows lift the head and back and return to the sitting position.

(viii) Then unwind the folded knee and be seated in the position of readiness for rest.

(ix) Rest for six to eight seconds and then repeat the *asana* with the same process.

Daily Practice

Do it three to four times. Never do it more than five times.

Benefits

This *asana* has some specific benefits for the people suffering from diabetes. Since this *asana* activizes all the cells of pancreas and increases its blood supply, it begins to function in a normal way. This *asana* has several other benefits. It corrects the disorders of the stomach, intestine, liver, kidneys, spleen and the organs of the abdominal area by activating and energizing them.

It has medicinal value for people suffering from indigestion, wind trouble, constipation and piles. Then disorders of the spine and joints are effectively corrected by this *asana*. It has also good effect on sex glands. It enhances sexual potentiality.

64

DHANUR ASANA

Position of Readiness

Lie down on your stomach. Keep your arms stretched on both sides. Place your head resting on any cheek on the floor. Bring the legs together and heels together. Breathe normally. Fold both the legs at the knees and bring the heels close to your hips. Then grab the right ankle with right hand and the left ankle with the left hand. In case you find it difficult to reach the ankles, you may hold the toes. Now holding either the ankles or the toes firmly, bring the knees and the ankles close together. Keep the cheek on the floor. You are now in position for performing *Dhanur Asana*.

Steps for Practice

(i) Inhale slowly but deeply and hold the breath.

(ii) When the inhaling is over, lift the head up and straighten it.

(iii) Without waiting any longer, give a backward pull with both the legs. Do it slowly but constantly and smoothly. Let the legs fly out backward as much as they can go. This will raise your chest, neck and head upwards.

(iv) Look towards the sky, keep the knees close to one another and on the floor. Do not lift the knees up from the floor. Keep the ankles together, if possible. Remain in this position for six to eight seconds while holding the breath. You should be as in Fig. 17.

(v) Start exhaling and simultaneously lowering the head and chest towards the floor.

(vi) Let your head rest on the floor, on either cheek, and also release the ankles and let them fall back slowly on the floor. Bring the hands also on the floor and relax. You have completed one round of *Dhanur Asana*.

(vii) After resting for six to eight seconds, repeat the *asana* with the same process as done during the first round.

Daily Practice

Do it three to four times only. Those who might find it

difficult to do the complete *asana* by holding both the ankles are advised to practise for a few days with only one ankle at a time.

In this case, the whole process of inhaling, raising up, holding and returning remains the same as done with both ankles. The only difference is that one leg remains stretched on the floor while the other is folded, held and pulled. It is very easy to do with one ankle at a time.

In this case, the whole process of inhaling, raising up, holding and returning remains the same as done with both ankles. The only difference is that one leg remains stretched on the floor while the other is folded, held and pulled. It is very easy to do with one ankle at a time.

Benefits

Dhanur Asana has several benefits. It activates all the glands of the endocrinal system. The pancreas get fully energized because of internal as well as external impact of this *asana* on it. There is thus an all round conditioning of the pancreas. As a result, its normal health is restored and it begins to release insulin in a proper way.

The *asana* has good effect on adrenal, thyroid, parathyroids, pituitary and the sex glands. Since the cells of all these glands are activated, the secretion of their respective hormones become normal.

It has curative and corrective effects on the disorders of the joints, spinal cord, lungs, chest and abdomen. It removes various types of stomach troubles, develops digestive power and takes off the extra weight and fat.

The *asana* has some specific benefits for women. It corrects menstrual and other troubles related to reproductive organs.

Proper Diet

It is important for the persons suffering from diabetes to avoid fried, fatty, spicy, starchy and sugar-containing food, for a period of four months from the date of starting yoga practices; the diabetic patients *should not take rice,* potato, banana, grapes, oranges, mangoes and such fruits in which the percentage of sugar is high. The sprouted grams(*ankurita chana*), *cheese or chhena* should be taken. They can take an apple a day. The non-vegetarians can add small quantities of fish, liver and eggs in their diet but should avoid meat or chicken for a few months.

It is generally found that diabetic people have extra weight. Their weight needs to be reduced to normal level. If they follow the principles and ways of taking proper diet as described in Chapter 1 and keep practising yoga, their extra weight will be automatically reduced. The point to remember is that they must take their evening meals at least two hours before going to bed and must always eat less than eight five per cent of their capacity. A diet chart for the diabetics is given below:

Breakfast (7 to 9 A.M.)

(i)   Apple—One or half or tomato juice (1 cup)
(ii) Germinated grams *(ankurit chana—1/4 cup)*
(iii) Whole-wheat bread or *chapati* (two-three pieces) with vegetables; or wheat *dalia;* or corn flakes with milk
(iv) Egg—One (boiled, poached or scrambled)
(v)   Tea or coffee—One cup (if preferred) without sugar.

Lunch and Dinner (12 to 2 P.M., 6 to 8 P.M.)

(i)   Salad (a mixture of cucumber, tomato, lettuce, radish, and some other green vegetables to be taken with either some salad dressing or salt, pepper and some lemon juice)
(ii)   Soup (Vegetable soup or any other kind)
(iii) Wheat bread.
(iv)   Pulse (*moong, masoor, chana*)
(v)   *Saag* (leafy vegetables of any kind)
(vi)   Green vegetables
(vii) For non-vegetarians—preferably fish or liver.

Afternoon Refreshment (3 to 5 P.M.)

(i)   Apple—half, or a few slices of papaya, or guava.

4

Asthma

ASTHMA IS popularly known in our country as *Dama*. The main trouble in this disease is breathlessness. The breathless condition of the patient is caused by the disorder and bronchial spasm in the respiratory system.

The most common symptom of this disease is that the patient feels difficulty in breathing. There is strain in exhaling the air. The asthmatic has to try hard for just getting a breath. In severe cases, the life of the patient becomes miserable and it makes him almost invalid. In medical terms the complicated condition of asthma is called Emphysema.

Asthma is mainly a disorder of the bronchioles. There is constriction of the bronchioles which disturbs the normal ratio of inspiration and expiration. Because of congestion of the blood vessels of the bronchial lining the expiration begins to get prolonged and difficult.

It is a widely prevalent disease of our time, affecting the young, old and even the children. In our country, millions suffer from this disease. The most disheartening aspect of asthma is that it does not get completely cured through medicines.

In treating the patient of asthma at the Indian Institute of Yoga. Patna, we have found very satisfactory results. The patients who followed our instructions well and practised yoga regularly were cured. We noticed that the health of both male and female patients became normal within a few months of their yoga practice and that there was no recurrence of it among the cured ones.

The yogic system of treatment of this disease necessitates doing three things: (i) regular practice of *pranayama* and select *asanas,* (ii) eating a proper diet, (iii) observance to certain principles and advice. Let me explain these.

Pranayama and Asanas

The selection of *pranayama* and *asanas* is made according to the need of the body in this *disease.* As already mentioned, the disease is primarily of the lungs and the respiratory system. Therefore, the *pranayama* and *asanas* have to be so selected as their practise would restore the normal health of the lungs and the whole of the respiratory system. Keeping this aim in view the following *pranayama* and *asanas* are recommended:

Ujjayee Pranayama

Ekpada Uttan Asana; Tara Asana; Yoga Mudra; Ushtra Asana; Simha Asana; Sarvang Asana; Matsya Asana; Padma Asana and Shava Asana.

The process of practising them will be presented one by one in the following pages.

Principles and Advice

It is most important that the asthmatics follow the following principles and advice in their diet and daily life. They must eat dinner at least two hours before going to bed at night. They should never eat more than 85 per cent of their capacity at any time. They should eat slowly and chew the food properly, should drink water after half an hour of finishing their meals, should take ten to twelve glasses of water in a day, and should avoid hot spices (*garam masala*), red pepper and pickles. Their intake of tea or coffee should not be more than two cups in a day. They should not take bed tea in the morning and they should not drink water upon arising and before going to toilet.

The asthmatics should avoid foods and ways of living which they have found to be allergic. They are advised to cut short or give up *zarda, cigarettes,* and the use of tobacco in any form. In case it is difficult to give up smoking, they should not smoke on empty stomach. They should sleep six to eight hours daily and try to be relaxed rather than tensed. The conditions which cause nervousness and tension should be corrected and eliminated. The asthmatics are strongly advised to bathe daily with cold or hot water, to rub the whole body with a rough towel, and to use bathing soap. They should avoid daily massaging the body with any oil. They should maintain neatness and cleanliness as much as possible. With these guidelines, they should practise the following *pranayamas* and *asanas:*

UJJAYEE PRANAYAMA
(IN LYING POSITION)

Before describing its stages of practice, a few words need to be told about what it is. *Pranayama* is mainly a *kriya* (exercise) with air. As we know air possesses several unique qualities. It contains life force *Prana Shakti*. It also has absorbing activating and massaging capacity. Because of these qualities, the air is regarded as a great purifier as well as a giver of life to the inner organs of the body. The body makes full use of these qualities of the air during *pranayama.*[1]

---

[1]For a comprehensive understanding of the scientific values of *pranayama* please see Dr. Phulgenda Sinha, *Yoga: Meaning, Values and Practice* (Patna: Indian Institute of Yoga, 1970) pp. 77-85; Swami Kuvalayananda, *Pranayama* (Bombay: Popular Prakashan, 1972).

Ujjayee Pranayama can be practised in two ways: (i) in standing position and (ii) in lying position. There is full impact of it in the first position and a little less in the second position. But the first is a little strenuous and the second is the easiest. Therefore, the practitioners are advised to practise *Ujjayee* in lying position first for a period of one month and then switch over to the standing position (as described next), if so preferred.

Position of Readiness

Lie down on your back on the floor. Make the body straight. Put the palms on the floor and close to the body. Bring the heels together and keep the legs loose. Look straight upward. Breathe normally.

Steps for Practice

There are altogether four steps in *Ujjayee:*
(i)   Exhaling air through the mouth;
(ii) Inhaling the air through both nostrils;
(iii) Retaining the air; and
(iv) Exhaling air again through the mouth.

These steps have to be performed in a sequence as described below:

(i) Exhale all the air of the body through mouth in a continuous and speedy way. The speed of air during exhalation is the same as it is when you whistle. The air is blown out through and between the lips without any twist on the facial tissues (see Fig. 18).

During this stage, the body should remain loose. There should be contraction of the abdominal area while exhaling the air. When all the air has been exhaled, the second stage begins without any delay.

(ii) Inhale air slowly with both nostrils. Do not rush. Let as much air be filled in the body as can be inhaled comfortably. Do not try to inhale excessively. Keep the body loose at this stage. The inhalation will make the abdominal area expanded.

(iii) When the inhalation is completed, retain the air inside and do the following steps: Bring the toes of both legs together and stretch them forward. Tighten the legs.

Pull the stomach gradually inwards. Keep the hands stretched. There should be a mild tightening of the muscles of the whole body. Be in this position (as shown in Fig. 19) for a period of three to four seconds only during the first week. Gradually increase the retaining time to six or eight seconds during the second or third week. The principle is to retain only as long as you can do it comfortably.

(iv) After retaining for the desired seconds, exhale the air through mouth in the same way as you did it during first step. The air should be released steadily and continuously but in a controlled way. Do not rush. While exhaling, start loosening the body muscles from top to downwards; that is, first loosen the chest, then the stomach, then the thighs, legs and the hands. Relax the whole body as you fully exhale. You have made one round of *Ujjayee Pranayama*. Now rest for five to six seconds.

During rest, just inhale and exhale through nostrils. When the resting is over, repeat the same process as done during the first round.

Daily Practice

On the first day of your practice, perform it only three times. Increase to four times on the second day and then to five times on the third day. Do not do it more than five times at a stretch. That is the maximum at one time. Those who wish to practise it twice a day, should give a gap of eight hours between the first and the second practice. Mornings and evenings are best for twice-a-day practice.

Caution

Pranayama must be done on empty stomach. Best time to do it is in the morning, after washing up. The second is in the evening. Those who would like to do it in the evening, must give a gap of three to four hours after lunch. it must be done where fresh air is available and when the body temperature is normal.

Benefits

Though a full description of its benefits is presented in

the following pages, let me mention here that the practice of *Ujjayee Pranayama* in the lying position has all the benefits as it has when done in the standing position. It is important to mention that it is safe and easy to do it in the lying position for any person of any age and of any bodily condition. People with high blood pressure, low blood pressure, people in the habit of taking drugs, and people with heart trouble are specially advised to practice it in this position till they feel quite normal.

UJJAYEE PRANAYAMA
(IN STANDING POSITION)

The method of practising *Ujjayee Pranayama* in lying position has been described earlier. Now its process of practising in standing position is presented. But let me first caution you.

Caution

Ujjayee Pranayama in standing position must be practised according to the requirements and methods described herein. Any laxity in following the instructions can cause injury and harm to the practitioner. Unless *Ujjayee Pranayama* in standing position is practised properly, the practitioner might fall on the ground and injure himself. Therefore, it is strongly advised to obey the following guidelines while practising *Ujjayee Pranayama* in standing position.

(i) Practise *Ujjayee Pranayama* first in lying position for about a month, then try in the standing position. There is no danger of injury and harm in lying position.

(ii) *Ujjayee Pranayama* in standing position must be practised in fresh air, when the body is not tired, when the body temperature is normal, and when the practitioner is not in a hurry.

(iii) Every step must be done gradually and in a rhythmical way.

Position of Readiness

Stand up and join your heels and spread your toes at an

angle of forty-degrees. Let the hands hang loosely on both sides. Look straight in front at the level of your eyes. Stand firm but without tightening the body. Be cheerful.

Steps for Practice

There are four steps in the standing position of *Ujjayee Pranayama:* (i) Exhaling air through mouth; (ii) Inhaling air through both nostrils, (iii) Retaining the air, and (iv) Exhaling the air again through mouth. These four steps have to be done in a sequence as described below:

(i) Exhale all air out through mouth in a speedy and continuous way. The air is blown out through and between the lips (see Fig. 18). The speed of exhaled air during this step is the same as it is when you whistle. During this stage keep the whole body loose. When you start exhaling, gradually pull the stomach muscles inside (contract the stomach). When all the air has been blown out, begin the second stage without any waiting.

(ii) Inhale slowly and continuously through both nostrils. Do not rush to finish inhaling quickly. Inhale without straining or twisting the facial muscles. Inhale only as much air as you can take quite comfortably. During inhalation, the body should remain loose. As air is filled inside, the abdominal muscles should expand. In other words let the abdominal area come forward as it happens when you blow air in a balloon.

(iii) When the inhaling is over, retain the air inside. For retaining, it is important that you start tightening the whole body gradually from legs upward to the chest. *Do not rush to retain all at once.* During retention the following process will be helpful for the conditioning of your body.

First tighten the muscles of the legs and then tighten the muscles of the thighs. Now gradually pull the stomach inside comfortably as much as you can. Raise the chest slightly forward. Bring the palms on the sides of thighs and tighten the hands and arms. Look in front at eye level. Do not raise the shoulders. Make a mild tight condition on the whole body. Do not tighten excessively. Retain the air inside for only as long as you feel comfortable. Do not

75

strain yourself too hard to hold the air (see Fig. 20). At the beginning stage of practice hold your breath for two to three seconds only and gradually increase the holding time to six or eight seconds. Holding breath for a very long time is not needed in *Ujjayee Pranayama*.

(iv) After holding the air for the specified time, exhale through mouth in a controlled but speedy manner. Along with exhaling, gradually start loosening the body from chest downwards to the legs. Do not loosen the body quickly. First loosen the chest, then the abdominal muscles, then the thighs, legs and hands. By the time you have completely exhaled, the body should also become loose. While exhaling do not bend the head or chest either backward or forward. Keep standing in a straight position. With this, one round of *Ujjayee* is completed. Now rest for six to eight seconds. During rest, just inhale and exhale twice through nostrils while keeping the mouth closed. When the resting time is over, repeat the same process for further rounds.

Daily Practice

Begin with only three on the first day. Make four rounds on the second day and go to five rounds on the third day. Five rounds are maximum. Do not ever practise more than five rounds in a single session.

Benefits

The most remarkable benefit of *Ujjayee* is that it does the internal purification, activation and energizing together with external control and conditioning all at the same time. For the asthmatics, *Ujjayee* is most effective for correcting and strengthening the condition of the lungs and the bronchiole linings. In order to convey its benefits properly let me explain what *Ujjayee* does to the internal organs of the body.

We know that air has an absorbing capacity. It can absorb certain things as moisture, fragrance and odour. Air has also force and power to carry things, such as, dust particles and even heavier things. We also know that if we put air in a balloon and give external pressure, the air would move and try to penetrate even the minutest available space. With this understanding about the nature of air it can very easily be comprehended that when air is kept in the body for a longer time, it absorbs the impurities of the system and when it is expelled with a force it carries those inner impurities out. Further, when external pressure is given it maximizes the inner penetration of the air and enables it to rub, activate and give inner masssage to the body cells and organs. This inner massage is a unique benefit of *Ujjayee* and hence recommended highly for any adult practitioner of yoga.

EKPADA UTTAN ASANA

In the preceding pages the methods of practising *Ujjayee Pranayama* has been fully explained. The asthmatics have been advised to practise five rounds of it daily in either lying or in standing position. After doing *Ujjayee*, the asthmatics should practise the selected *asanas* as presented in this chapter. The first *asana* of this series is *Ekpada Uttan Asana*. Its method of practice is explained below.

Position of Readiness

Lie down on your back on the floor. Make the body straight. Bring the heels together. Keep the palms nearer to the body on the floor. Let the body remain loose. Look straight upward. Breathe normally.

Steps for Practice

(i) Stretch out the toes of any one leg and make it hard and tight all along. Keep the other leg loose.

(ii) When the leg has been tightened, start inhaling and raising it upward towards the sky. Inhale and raise the leg slowly, so that it should take about eight seconds to bring it upward in a perpendicular position. While lifting the leg upwards do not twist or turn the other parts of the body. Let the whole body remain on the floor. Lift the leg only as high as it can go comfortably. Do not give excessive strain in pushing the leg upwards.

(iii) When the leg has been brought up to a maximum height, hold the breath and keep the leg firmly in standing position. Retain the breath for six seconds only. During this stage of retention see that your body is straight; the lifted leg is quite tight, palms are down on the floor; and you are looking upwards as shown in Fig. 21.

(iv) After holding the breath for six seconds, start exhaling and lowering the leg towards the floor. It should take about eight seconds to complete exhalation. The leg should remain hard and tight while it is brought down. When the leg comes to the floor, the round of *Ekpada Uttan Asana* is completed.

(v) Now rest for six to eight seconds. After the resting time is over, start with the other leg by following the same process.

Daily Practice

Begin with four rounds. Do it alternately. Gradually increase to six rounds.

Benefits

For the asthmatics it has a curative effect. During retention the air penetrates the bronchioles and activates their linings in a mild way. As a result of this inner activation, its power is increased and its health is restored.

This *asana* has several other benefits. It brings flexibility to the hip joints and corrects disorders of the stomach and intestine. It removes wind troubles and gastric condition of the digestive system.

It tones up the muscles of the sex-glands and enhances their potency. For women it has a curative effect on menstrual disorders. It is easy to do and hence recommended to all practitioners of yoga.

TARA ASANA

Position of Readiness

Stand up by making a forty-five degree angle with the feet. Let the hands hang loosely on the sides. Keep the body straight and look in front at the level of the eyes. Breathe normally. This is the position of readiness.

Steps for Practice

Before describing the steps it needs to be pointed out that it is a *kriya* of the hands and the arms. In this *kriya* hands are folded six times according to the following process:

(i) Make the hands tight and gradually raise them in front while inhaling. By the time the hands have been brought in front on the level of the shoulders, inhaling should be completed. Now hold the breath. Keep the palms upwards. Keep the hands straight, parallel and firm. This is the first fold as shown in Fig. 22.

(ii) After giving a pause for a second on the first fold, turn the palms downward and move the hands on their respective sides. During this second fold, let the hands come at level with the shoulders in such a way that they are in one line. Keep looking straight in front while holding the breath as shown in Fig. 23.

(iii) After giving a pause for a second on the second fold, bring the hands again in front keeping the palms downward. Keep the hands tightened and parallel to one another. The distance between the hands should be six inches for teenagers and eight inches for adults. Give a pause for a second on this fold.

(iv) Then turn the palms to face one another and lift them tightly towards the sky. The palms should face one another when fully raised upwards and the distance between them should be six to eight inches (see Fig. 24). Keep looking straight forward. Do not bend the body. Stay in that position for only a second.

(v) Now twist the palms facing downward and bring the hands to the sides as you were in the second fold (Fig. 23). Palms are downwards. Hands are tightened and they are straight in one line. Stay there for a second. You have to hold the breath upto this fold.

(vi) Then start exhaling and slowly lowering the hands down. When the hands have returned to the sides, you should have exhaled completely. Now loosen the body and

79

rest. Let the hands hang loosely. You have completed one round of *Tara Asana*. After resting for two deep breaths make more rounds by following the same process.

Daily Practice

Do it only three times a day during the first week. During the second week and after, increase to four times daily. Five times is maximum in a day.

Benefits

Tara Asana has a good strengthening effect upon the lungs and chest. Though the outward activation in this *kriya* is of hands, it brings internal activation of the lungs, muscles of the chest and the respiration system. For the asthmatics, therefore, it provides a corrective as well as strengthening effect to their bronchioles and lungs.

For the general practitioners *Tara Asana* has several benefits. It enhances the measurement of the chest. Those whose chest is not properly developed can find it more rewarding for making it proportionate. It builds up the muscles of the chest in an all round way and has a curative effect of any disorders of that area.

Those who wish to add a few inches to their height might also find it very rewarding. People suffering from pain in their shoulder-joints can correct these disorders through *Tara Asana*. It is easy to do. People of any age group can do it.

YOGA MUDRA

Position of Readiness

The perfect way of practising *Yoga Mudra* is to be in the Lostus Pose first. But it is not easy for everyone to make the Lotus Pose. Hence those who cannot make it should sit down on the floor with folded legs. After being seated either in the Lotus or in *Sukh Asana* (as shown in Fig. 1 and Fig. 2) do the following steps. Bring both the hands at the back. Grab the wrist of one hand with the other hand. Make a fist with the hand which has been grabbed. At this stage keep the hands loose and let them rest on the back.

Keep the spine straight. Look in front while keeping the neck and head straight upward. This is the position of readiness.

Steps for Practice

(i) Exhale gradually and simultaneously, start lowering the head towards the ground. You have to synchronize exhaling with the bending of upper area of the body towards the ground. Let the head come down only as far as it can easily be lowered. Do not give excessive strain to the spine while lowering the head. If possible, touch the ground with the forehead. By the time the head has touched the ground all air should have been completely exhaled.

(ii) After touching the ground or only going down as much as possible, retain the breath. Now tighten the hands and gradually raise them (in grabbed form) upwards as high as possible without excessive strain. Remain in this position for six to eight seconds as shown in Fig. 25.

(iii) Start inhaling while lowering down the hands and gradually return to the position of readiness. Loosen the hands and the body. Rest for six to eight seconds. After resting, make a few more rounds by following the same process.

Daily Practice

Make only two rounds daily during the first week and increase it to four rounds during the second week. Its four rounds are the maximum.

Benefits

It activates and exercises the lungs and their bronchial branches in a very effective way. Because of reverse conditioning of the upper area of the body, the blood from the lower region begins to flow upwards and massages the veins of the lower bronchioles of the lungs. This helps restore the normal health of the lungs and their functioning. For these reasons *Yoga Mudra* has a curative effect for the asthmatics.

81

For the general practitioners, *Yoga Mudra* provides several benefits. It corrects the disorders of the spine; removes gastric troubles and constipation; strengthens the digestive system; and enhances sexual potentiality.

USHTRA ASANA

Position of Readiness

You need to have something soft underneath the knees for making this *asana*. Put a blanket or a towel on the floor. First be seated on the soft floor. Fold the legs at the knees and keep them apart from one another at about six inches. Then stand on the knees and let the ankles and toes of both legs fall flat on the floor. Keep the heels about six inches apart. Now the back of the knees, the calves and the heels would be in an upward position. This is the position of readiness for *Ushtra Asana*.

Steps for Practice

(i) Kneel and catch hold of the back of the ankles of right leg with the right hand. Hold it firmly. If you cannot reach above the heel, you may just catch the heels.

(ii) Now catch hold of the heel or the back of the left ankle with the left hand. Make the grip firm.

(iii) Holding the heels or the back of the ankles, straighten the thighs and waist. Bend the head and neck backwards as much as you can. Push the waist area slightly forward. Breathe normally and stay in that position for six to eight seconds as shown in Fig. 26.

(iv) After holding for the desired seconds, return to the position of readiness with the following process:

Release the left hand first and straighten up the left side of the body a little. Then release the right hand and make the body straight and in the kneeling position. If possible, sit down on the soles and in between the heels and then rest. You have completed one round of *Ushtra Asana*.

(v) After resting for six to eight seconds make some more rounds by following the same process.

Daily Practice

Do it only twice daily during the first week. During the second week and afterwards repeat it a maximum of four times daily.

Benefits

For the asthmatics *Ushtra Asana* brings a good effect upon the whole of respiratory system. This *asana* activates the facial tissues; the nasal passage, the pharynx, the lungs and the whole of respiratory organs and the nerves. Because of internal as well as external activation during this *asana,* the weakened condition of the organs of respiration is corrected and their normal health is restored.

Ushtra Asana has several benefits for the general practitioners. It corrects many disorders of the neck, shoulders, and the spine. It cures various types of visionary defects of the eyes and strengthens all the sense organs. People suffering from throat trouble, tonsil, voice defect and chronic headache will find this *asana* very beneficial. It has also a good conditioning effect upon the muscles of the chest and in making the chest area proportionate in size. It is not a difficult *asana.* With a little practice any person can do it.

SIMHA ASANA

Position of Readiness

Put a blanket or a towel on the floor. Fold back both the legs at the knees and be seated on the curve of soles and toes, keeping the heels apart and turned upwards under the hips. Since it might be difficult for some persons to make this curve with the toes, soles and heels, they are advised to sit on their folded legs in any position they can possibly manage to make.

After being seated either on the curve of heels or in any position, do the following things: Make the body straight. Keep the head, the neck and the spine in one line. Look in front. Put the palms on their respective side knees. Breathe normally. This is the position of readiness of *Simha Asana.*

Steps for Practice

(i) Start exhaling partially through both nostrils and partially through mouth and at the same time start extending out the tongue. Do not rush. Protrude the tongue in a straightforward position gradually. Let the tongue come out fully. By the time the tongue has been pushed out, the exhalation should be over. Then hold the breath.

(ii) When the tongue is fully out, do the following steps. Spread out the fingers of both hands and tighten them. Stretch the eyes and make them look frightening. Keep the whole body tight. Stay in this tight and strained condition for about six to eight seconds. You are in the *Simha Asana* as shown in Fix. 27.

(iii) After holding the *asana* for a few seconds, start inhaling and withdrawing the tongue. Let the body be gradually loosened while inhaling and pulling back the tongue. When the tongue has been fully withdrawn, close the mouth and breathe normally and rest for a few seconds. Let the whole body relax, while being seated in the same position.

(iv) After resting for six to eight seconds make a few more rounds by following the same process.

Daily Practice

Begin with two rounds daily during the first week. From the second week onwards make four rounds daily. Do not make more than four rounds in a single sitting. In certain cases this *asana* can be performed twice daily after a gap of eight hours between the first and the second sittings.

Benefits

Simha Asana is very famous for its various remarkable benefits. It has medicinal value for curing throat trouble, voice deficiency and tonsillitis.

It has also good effect on the respiratory system. It activates the larynx, trachea and all the bronchioles. It provides an invigorative effect on the thyroid cartileges. Because of this internal activation and invigoration, there is restoration of health in the whole of respiratory system and its disorder is removed. This is an easy *asana*. Any person can do it.

SARVANGA ASANA

Position of Readiness

Lie down on your back on the floor. Keep the palms down and nearer to the body. Bring the heels and toes together and keep them loose. Make the whole body straight and look towards the ceiling. Breathe normally. This is the position of readiness.

Steps for Practice

(i) Stretch out the toes of both legs and make them tight. Then start inhaling and at the same time start lifting both the legs together towards the ceiling. Inhale in such a way that by the time the legs have been brought to a prependicular position, inhaling is completed.

(ii) Just when the inhaling is completed and both the legs have been brought fully upward, bring both the palms under the hip, and raise the whole body upward by pushing it with both hands while exhaling. During this second stage do the following things: Raise the body upward in a gradual way. Let the hands help in pushing up the body. Do not try to raise the body with any excessive strain. Go only as high as the condition of your body permits (see Fig. 28). Keep both the palms on both sides of the back for support. When the body has been raised to a maximum point (as shown in Fig. 29), stay there and breathe normally. Make the legs tight and keep them together. Stay in this position for ten to fifteen seconds during the first week. Gradually develop the time to one minute in a month and upto three minutes during the second month.

(iii) After standing on the shoulders for the desired seconds or minutes, return to the ground according to the following method: Fold the legs at the knees first. This will bring the heels on the hip. Now gradually move the

85

palms towards the hip and let the body come down slowly on the floor. While returning, support the body's weight with hands. Make it a smooth return. When the hip touches the ground, drop the heels nearer the hip first. Put the palms on the floor on both sides of the body. Then stretch out the legs and let them fall on the floor. You have made one round of *Sarvanga Asana*. Now rest. (iv) Rest for about ten seconds. During rest breathe in a normal way.

Daily Practice

Sarvanga Asana is done only once. It is not a repeatable *asana*. The difference is in the timing of holding. Those who have practised this *asana* for more than a month can hold it for three minutes. The maximum time for holding it is three minutes. The beginners should start it with ten seconds only and should increase the time gradually.

Benefits

Sarvanga Asana is one of the most valued *asana* of the Hatha Yoga system. As its name indicates it is indeed an *asana* of the whole body. There is hardly any area of the body which is not energized, activated and exercised during this *asana*. Because of its wholesome effect, it is regarded next only to the king of all *asanas* — *Shirsha Asana*.

For the asthmatics, *Sarvanga Asana* has medicinal value. It exercises all the bronchioles and the totality of the lungs. It removes the weakening condition of the lungs through internal activation. Since the whole of respiratory system is invigorated and strengthened during this *asana*, the troubles of the lungs are corrected.

This *asana* has countless benefits. Therefore it is a very desirable *asana* for the general practitioners. It corrects any disorder of the circulatory system; supplies blood to the facial tissues; removes constipation, gastric disorders, and abdominal troubles; strengthens the digestive system and energizes all the sex glands. It is good for both male and female practitioners.

MATSYA ASANA

The method of practising *Sarvanga Asana* has been described in the preceding pages. After practising *Sarvanga Asana* it is necessary to practise *Matsya Asana*. The need for doing *Matsya* after *Sarvanga* is for some good reasons. Certain *asanas* activate certain parts of the body more than the others. In order to reverse this difference of impact, such *asanas* are followed by parcticular *asanas* to create a balanced effect. For example, during *Sarvanga Asana* the head, the neck and the shoulders become passive and the lower areas of the body become active. In order to create a balance, *Sarvanga* is followed by *Matsya Asana* so that the head, the neck and the shoulders become active and the lower areas of the body remain passive. Thus by doing the *Matsya Asana* after the *Sarvanga Asana*, activation of the whole body is done properly and in a balanced way.

There are two ways of doing the *Matsya Asana:*

(i) With the Lotus Pose, and (ii) without being in the Lotus Pose.

Though the first form is regarded superior to the second; basically both are equally beneficial. Since it is not possible for everyone to make Lotus Pose, both forms are described so that every person can practise it.

Position of Readiness

Make any one of the following two positions:

(i) Be in the Lotus Pose. Then lie down on your back while keeping the legs folded in Lotus form. After making the spine, neck and head fall on the floor completely, let the thighs also fall down. Put the hands on the floor nearer to the body. Keep the palms down. Breathe normally. This is the position of readiness with Lotus Pose. If you cannot do this, try the second method as described below:

(ii) Lie down on the floor on your back. Fold the legs at the knees and bring the heels near the hips. Keep the knees together and let the heels be separated from one another at about four inches. Put the palms on the floor. Make the body straight. Look upward and breathe normally. This is the easy way of readiness.

Steps for Practice

Bring the palms under the thighs. Now you have to do several things. While giving a pull on the thighs, lift the head slightly upward. Let the weight of the upper areas of the body rest on the elbows. Then bend the head backward and make an arch by bending the backbone. When the arch (curve) is made, put the head to rest on the floor. For making a bigger arch give more pull on the thighs and more twist on the neck and back. But do not give excessive pull. In the beginning start with a minimum pull.

(ii) When the arch has been made according to the suitability of your body condition, stay there in that form. If you are in Lotus Pose, then grab the toes of the left leg with the right hand and that of the right leg with the left hand and give a light pull on them as shown in Fig.30. In case you are doing the *Matsya Asana* the easy way without the Lotus Pose, then stretch out both the hands on the side of the body and keep the palms on the floor as shown in Fig.31.

(iii) Now make a few deep but slow and gradual breathings. Stay in this position for about six to eight seconds. This makes the *Matsya Asana* completely done.

After being in *Matsya Asana* for the desired period return to the position of readiness with the following process: In case you were holding the toes, leave them and bring the palms down on the floor. Then pull the thighs with your hands again by making a fold at the elbows. Now lift the head upwards and strengthen the neck and head. Then gradually bring the back, shoulders, neck and head on the floor, unfold the legs and stretch them on the floor and rest.

(v) Rest for two to three normal breaths. After the rest is over, make one or two more rounds by following the same process.

Benefits

For the asthmatics, *Matsya Asana* has several benefits. It

Fig 13 Ardhavakra Asana

Fig 14 Matsyendra Asana

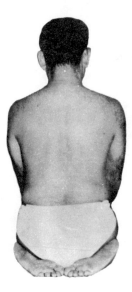

Fig 15 Suptavajra Asana (Position of Readiness)

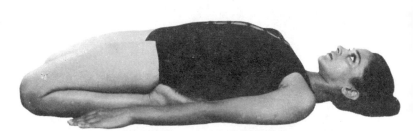

Fig 16 Suptavajra Asana

Fig 17 Dhanur Asana

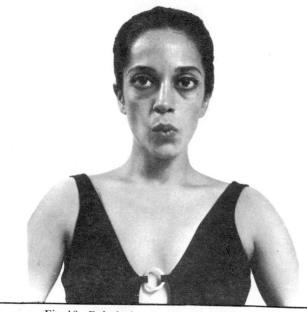

Fig 18 Exhalation in Ujjayee Pranayama

Fig 19   Retention in Ujjayee in Lying Position

Fig 20   Retention in Ujjayee
in Standing Position

Fig 21   Ekpada Uttan Asana

Fig 22   Hands in Front for Tara Asana

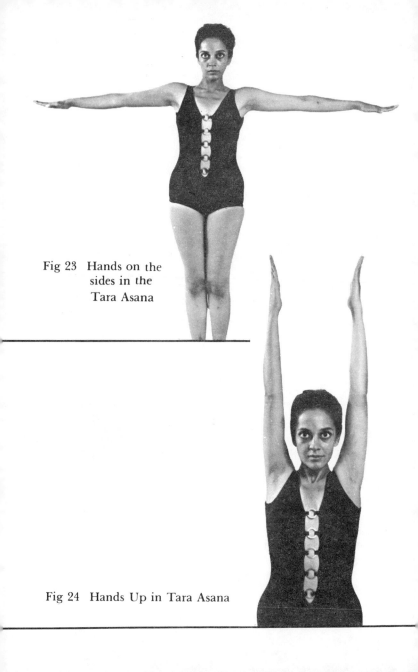

Fig 23   Hands on the
            sides in the
            Tara Asana

Fig 24   Hands Up in Tara Asana

Fig 25   Yoga Mudra

Fig 26 Ushtra Asana

corrects the disorders of the respiratory system as a whole. This is because all the organs concerned with respiration, such as, the nasal passage, the pharynx, the larynx, the trachea, the bronchi and the lungs are well exercised during this *asana*.

Matsya Asana provides several other benefits. It has a good effect on the facial tissues. It activates the spine and all the muscles of the back. As a result of this activation the disorders of the spine and back are corrected. It removes stiffness of the neck and back and brings flexibility in the whole upper area of the body. It has a good effect upon their malfunctioning.

Its easy form can be practised by any person of any age group, since it is a highly beneficial *asana,* it is recommended to all practitioners of yoga.

Proper Diet

The asthmatics should eat a balanced diet which includes salad, fresh fruits, green vegetables, germinated gram and *saag* (leafy vegetables) in their daily meals. They should eat four time a day, that is, breakfast, lunch, afternoon refreshment and dinner.

The breakfast should consist of some fruit juice, fresh fruits, a handful of germinated gram, wheat bread and green vegetables.

The lunch and dinner should begin with salad. (slices of cucumber, lettuce, tomato, carrot, beets, and any vegetable which can be eaten raw). Salad eaten should be about a cupful mixed with salt, pepper and lemon juice or with salad dressing. After eating salad, they should eat soup (if possible), wheat bread, pulse (except *arhar*), any kind of *saag* and some fresh green vegetables. The non-vegetarians can eat fish and liver if they like. Meat of any type should be avoided for a period of three months.

In the afternoon, some light refreshment should be taken, such as, fresh fruits, cheese, cake, *halwa* or salted biscuits.

97

5

Arthritis
Inflammation of Joints

ARTHRITIS IS a disease of the joints. People suffering from this disease have a burning feeling, terrible pain and aching in their affected joints. There is swelling, redness, stiffness, and heat in the joints. There are several variations of arthritis. The most common types are the Rheumatoid arthritis, Gout and Osteoarthritis.

It is difficult to explain the root cause of all these kinds of arthritis as there are various reasons for it. For example, it could be due to a lack of proper diet, lack of proper exercise, lack of hygienic care, due to poor health and similar other factors.

In our country millions of people suffer from this vexing, torturous and disabling disease. It affects both male and female of all age groups. The most disheartening aspect of the disease is that it does not get easily cured through medicine when it is in chronic stages.

It is a common practice all over the world to give medicines and recommend physical exercises to the patients for curing this disease. Since therapeutic yoga is not yet well known to the medical practitioners they do not make use of it to cure arthritis.

In treating the patients of arthritis at our Institute we have found that regular practise of some selected yoga *asanas* cures this disease within two months when it is of moderate type. In chronic cases it takes four to five months or more to cure and restore normal health. The most remarkable aspect of yoga treatment is that it cures the disease without the use of any medicine and it gives a permanent cure. Let me now explain the yogic system of treatment.

Yogic Treatment

The arthritic or rheumatic patients have to do three things:

(i) Regular practice of selected yoga *asanas*, (ii) to take proper diet, and (iii) to maintain proper hygienic care. A detailed description of these aspects is explained below:

Yoga Asana

The arthritics are advised to practise *Santulan Asana, Trikona Asana, Veera Asana, Gomukh Asana, Briksha Asana, Setubandh Asana, Siddha Asana, Natraj Asana, and Shava Asana*. The method of practising these *asanas* is presented one by one in the following pages. A regular practice of these *asanas* will cure arthritis of any type without the use of any medicine. Those who are used to taking medicine are advised to stop it after they have practised Yoga for two to three weeks.

SANTULAN ASANA

Position of Readiness

Put a carpet or blanket or mat on the floor. Stand up on the carpeted floor. Make the body straight and firm. Look straight forward. Let the hands hang on the sides. This is the position of readiness.

Note : For doing this *asana* you have to stand on one leg at a time. It is not easy for everyone to stand on one leg on the floor. Therefore, those who might have any difficulty in standing on one leg on the floor, should stand near a pillar or a wall for supporing the body weight.

Steps for Practice

(i) Stand up on the right leg and fold the left leg at the knee. Bring the heel of the left leg near the hip. If the heel cannot be brought nearer the hip due to pain in the knee, fold the leg backward as much as possible.

(ii) Catch the toes of the left leg with the left hand in such a way that all the toes are held with the palm. Bring heel of the folded leg to the hip or nearer to it.

(iii) Tighten the right hand. Keep all the fingers together and slowly raise the right hand up towards the sky. Do not rush in lifting the hand. Keep the palm facing downwards, while raising the hand. When the hand is fully raised the palm should remain in the straight forward position.

(iv) Stay in that position for six to eight seconds. Keep the lifted hand tight and firm. The right leg on which you are standing should be tight and straight. Keep looking straight. There is no special breathing requirement in this *asana*. Keep breathing normally, while doing this *asana* (as shown in Fig. 32).

(v) After staying in this position for six to eight seconds, return to the position of readiness with the following process. Slowly bring the lifted hand down, keeping it in a tight condition. Do not drop the hand. When the raised hand has reached the side, release the left leg to come on the floor. You are now in the position of readiness again after completing one round of *Santulan Asana*.

After resting for six seconds stand on the left leg and fold the right leg and raise the left hand in the same way as you did the first time. Make further rounds alternately by following the same process.

Daily Practice

Do it only four times daily during the first week. After practising for a week, increase to six times a day.

Benefits

Santulan Asana is mainly a *kriya* of the major joints of the body. It removes rigidity and brings flexibility to them. It also normalizes the blood circulation in the affected areas and tones up the muscles. As a result of enhanced blood circulation, flexibility and muscular conditioning, pain in the joints is corrected.

This *asana* has curative effect upon the knees, ankles, shoulder joints, wrists, palms and fingers. It is an easy *asana* and any person can practise it either standing on the floor or with the help of the wall. For the general practitioners it is a good *asana* for their body activation and flexibility of the joints

TRIKONA ASANA

Position of Readiness

Stand up on the floor. Keep the legs at about two and a half feet distance from one another. Look in front. Let the hands hang loosely on the sides. Make the legs firm and tight.

Steps for Practice

(i) Inhale slowly and at the same time raise both the hands up to the level of the shoulders on their respective sides. Keep the hands tight while raising up. This will bring both the hands in one line. The palms should be facing downwards. By the time hands have come up in one line, inhaling should be completed. Stay there for two seconds as shown in Fig. 33.

(ii) Then start exhaling and simultaneously lower the left hand to touch the left foot and raise the right hand up towards the sky. By the time you have touched the foot you shall complete exhaling. When exhaling is over hold the breath. While going down bend forward, not sideways.

Keep looking at the toes you are going to touch. Try to touch the toes of the left foot. After touching the toes, turn your head right and raise it towards the sky. Now try to see the palm of the right hand. Keep looking at the right palm for about two seconds. Do not bend your legs at the knees. Keep the legs quite tight (see Fig. 34 for this second phase).

(iii) After looking at the right palm for a few seconds bring the upper hand tightly in front and then look at the floor beneath that palm. During this stage your left hand remains on the toes of the left foot and your right hand is fully stretched out in front of you. Your body is bent right in front. Legs are quite tight. The right arm is closer to the right temple. You are still holding the breath and your posture is as shown in Fig. 35.

(iv) Then move the right hand about forty-five degrees to the right side while keeping the arm and the hand quite stretched. At this stage the fingers of the right hand are together and the palm about one foot above the ground. Look at the ground where the fingers of the right hand are pointing as shown in Fig. 36. Stay in this position for two seconds. Keep holding the breath.

Now bring the right hand on the right leg and start inhaling and standing up, your hands are dragged lightly on the legs till you are back in the standing position. After returning to the position of readiness your hands are again on the sides. You have completed one round of *Trikona Asana*. Now rest for two normal breaths.

(v) After resting for about five seconds repeat the *asana* by following the same process. In the second round you have to touch the right foot and raise the left hand towards the sky. Make further rounds alternately.

Daily Practice

Make four alternate rounds daily during the first week. During the second week and afterwards make six rounds daily. Never make more than eight rounds in a single day.

Benefits

Trikona Asana has medicinal value for curing the pain or any disorder of the neck and the shoulder joints. People suffering from stiffness in the neck will find this *asana* very effective in correcting that disorder.

This *asana* has good effect upon the spine, the hip joints, the hands and the palms. All the major joints above the waist area are properly activated and their muscles are duly toned up by this *asana*. The arthritics are advised to practise *Santulan Asana* first and then the *Trikona Asana*. By doing them one after the other all the major and minor joints of the body are fully activated and their functioning is normalized.

For the general practitioners, *Trikona Asana* has several benefits. It develops the visionary power of the eyes; brings flexibility to the spine; and provides the quality of mental attentiveness. It is an easy *asana* and hence recommended to all practitioners of yoga.

VEERA ASANA

Position of Readiness

Be seated on the floor in an easy way. Keep the body straight upward. Look in front, at the level of the eyes. Breathe normally.

Steps for Practice

(i) Fold one leg at the knee and bring its heel behind the hips. The toes of this leg should fall on the ground. The heel is up, touching the hip. There is no body weight on the folded leg, all the weight of the body is on the floor.

(ii) Now fold the other leg at the knee and bring this foot on the thigh of the folded leg. Let the knee of this leg fall on the floor and let its sole rest on the thigh of the other leg.

(iii) Stretch both the hands on their respective sides and then bring the wrists on the head. Then join the palms and the fingers of both hands close together. Keep the wrists on top of the head and keep the fingers straight upward. Then try to straighten the elbows on their respective sides as much as is comfortably possible.

(iv) Now straighten the spine, the neck and the head. Look in front. Keep the palms and the fingers together.

103

Your elbows should remain straight and tight. Keep breathing in a normal way. You are in *Veera Asana*. Stay in this position for eight seconds, as shown in Fig. 37.

(v) After eight seconds, unfold the palms and bring down the hands. Then lift the upper foot by hand and bring it down on the floor. Then pull back the other folded leg and bring it to an easy pose. Now rest for five seconds. You have completed one round of *Veera Asana*. Do more rounds alternately. In other words, during the second round, first the leg, which was up, will be folded backward, and then the other foot will be put on its thigh.

Daily Practice

Do four rounds daily. It might be increased to a maximum of six rounds. Do not practise more than six rounds in a single day.

Benefits

Veera Asana exercises all the major and minor joints in a single process in a very effective way. The external activation enhances the blood circulation in the joint areas and restores their normal health.

This *asana* has also a good strengthening effect on the lungs and the chest. It tones up the muscles of the thighs, the hip and the arms and takes away the fat from these areas.

It has also symbolic value. It is held that those practising *Veera Asana* will develop courage, boldness and bravery.

GOMUKH ASANA

Position of Readiness

The proper position of readiness for *Gomukh Asana* might be difficult to make for those arthritics whose knees, ankles and toes are severly affected. Therefore, such patients are advised to sit on the floor by simply folding the legs at the knees and keeping the spine straight.

Those who can make the position of readiness should sit on the floor according to the following steps: Make a kneeling position on the floor by keeping the body weight on both the knees. Keep the knees separated from one another by about four inches. Let the ankles and toes of both the legs fall on the floor in such a way that the toes are brought close to one another but the heels are upwards, spread out.

This will make an arch-like curve with the toes, soles and the heels. Then gradually sit down on the curve of the soles by putting the whole weight of the body on it. Put the palms on the thigh. Look in front at the level of your eyes. Keep the spine quite straight. You are now in the perfect position of readiness of *Gomukh Asana* (See Fig. 38).

Steps for Practice

(i) Slowly bring right hand to the back. Fold it at the right elbow and then raise the back of the palm up towards the neck. This will keep the back of the palm pressed against the spine. Let the fingers of the right hand face upwards. Keep the right hand firmly in that position.

(ii) Now fold your left hand at the elbow and raise it upwards by putting the left palm on the left shoulder. Then, first try to touch the fingers of the left hand with the right hand. Some people might have difficulty in even touching the fingers. They should make the move as much as possible and then stay there. Those who do not have any difficulty in touching the fingers should make a lock by folding the fingers of both the hands. For making the lock the fingers are slightly crooked and then these crooks may be hooked together and pulled against each other.

(iii) After making the lock with the fingers of both hands, try to raise the elbow of the left hand straight upwards. Keep the spine firm and straight. Look in front. Breathe normally. Stay in this locked position for six to eight seconds. Those who cannot make the lock should exert to attain this position as much as possible and then should stay there for six to eight seconds in the same position. When the fingers of one hand are locked against the fingers of the other hand in that sitting position it makes the *Gomukh Asana* perfectly completed as shown in Fig. 38.

(iv) After staying in that position for six to eight seconds, loosen the grip on the fingers and then unlock the fingers gradually. Then slowly bring both the hands on the thighs and rest. You have made one round of *Gomukh Asana*. After resting for two normal breaths make more rounds alternately by following the same process. That means you have to bring now the left hand on the back and raise the elbow of the right hand.

Daily Practice

Make four rounds daily during the first week. During the second week and afterwards make six rounds daily. Do it alternately.

Benefits

Gomukh Asana has, as a single exercise, a corrective effect upon all the major and minor joints of the body. It exercises the finger joints, the elbows, the shoulder joints, the toes, the ankles, the knees and the hip joints very effectively. All the muscles and nerves related to various joints are automatically toned up, activated and normalized.

Because of activation of the muscles of the joints, blood circulation is improved in those areas. As a result, the waste products are removed from the joints. It restores the synovial fluid (joint fluid) and thereby removes spasticity and pain.

For the general practitioners, this *asana* has various good results. It brings flexibility in the joints, strengthens the bones, increases the measurement of the chest, and enhances the strength of the lungs and heart.

VRIKSHA ASANA

Position of Readiness

Stand up on the floor. Look in front at the level of your eyes. Keep the hands hanging loose on the sides. Make the body straight and firm. Breathe normally. This is the position of readiness.

Steps for Practice

You have to stand up on one leg for practising this *asana*. In case you have difficulty in standing on one leg, take the support of a wall or a pillar. Then do the following steps:

(i) Stand up on the left leg and fold back the right leg at the knee. Bring the right foot on the thigh of the left leg so that the outer part of the heel and sole rest on the left thigh. This will twist the right foot a little and press its side against the left thigh. Do not press the thigh with the heel itself but with its side. When the side of the heel has been firmly pressed against the left thigh, make the left leg and the whole body tight and straight.

(ii) Then raise both hands sideways towards the head. When the hands are stretched above the head, join the palms and the fingers together. Then bring the palms on the head so that the wrists rest on the head.

(iii) When the palms have been jointly put on the head, you have to do several things at this stage. Try to give a backward pull on the folded elbows in order to bring them in one line. But do not exert too much. Look straight forward at the level of your eyes. Tighten the leg you are standing on. Now there is tightness all over the body. You are breathing normally, stay in that position for six to eight seconds. You are in *Vriksha Asana,* as shown in Fig. 39.

(iv) After holding in that *asana* for the desired period, loosen the pressure on the palms and stretch out the arms in order to bring them back tightly to their respective sides. When the hands are in position, grab the toes of the folded leg, lift it slightly upwards and then drop it on the floor. You are now back in the position of readiness. Rest for two normal breaths.

(v) After resting for a few seconds, repeat the *asana* a few more times alternating with leg positions. For example, in the second round you have to stand up on the right leg and fold the left leg. Then follow the various steps done in the first round for completing this *asana*.

Daily Practice

Make four rounds daily during the first week. During the second week and afterwards make six rounds daily. Keep alternating the leg while making further rounds. Do not practise it more than six rounds in a single day.

Benefits

Vriksha Asana activates all the joints of the body. All the major joints of the body are affected by this single *asana*. It tones up the muscles of the ankles, toes, knees, hip joints, shoulder joints, elbows, hands and fingers. As a result of this activation and conditioning of the joint muscles, blood circulation becomes normal in the joints and they regain strength.

For the general practitioners *Vriksha Asana* has good conditioning and strengthening effect upon their bodily joints and bones. It brings flexibility in the legs and hands and enhances the measurement of the chest. It is an easy *asana* and hence every practitioner of Yoga can do it.

SETUBANDHA ASANA

Position of Readiness

Lie down on your back on the floor. Fold the legs at the knees and bring the heels near the hip. Keep the heels at about two to three inches apart from one another. Let the knees also be from one another by about three inches. Bring your hands closer to the body on both sides. Put the palms on the floor. Look straight up. Breathe normally. This is the position of readiness.

Steps for Practice

(i) Lift the hip and the waist upwards while keeping the shoulders and the feet on the floor. When the hip has been raised upwards, support it with the palms on both sides.

(ii) Gradually keep raising the hip upwards while pushing the palms towards the waist area. Let the hands help in raising the waist upwards as high as it can be raised without strain. Now support the body weight on the thumbs and the index fingers and the palms on sides. Let the shoulders, neck and the head be firmly on the floor. Try to check that the thighs are parallel to one another with a gap of about three inches. Keep breathing normally. Stay in this position for six to eight seconds, as shown in Fig. 40.

(iii)After remaining in the raised up position of six to eight seconds, start lowering the hip towards the floor while still supporting the body weight on the palms, but do not let the body drop on the floor. Bring it down slowly. When the hip, the waist and the back are on the floor put your palms on the floor on both sides of the body. Stretch out the legs on the floor and rest for two to three normal breaths.

(iv) After resting for a few seconds repeat the *asana* by following the same process as you did during the first round.

Daily Practice

Make four rounds daily during the first week. During the second week and afterwards make a maximum of six rounds. Do not ever make more than six rounds in a day.

Benefits

The main impact of *Setubandha Asana* is on the spine and the hip joints. Those who have pain either in any part of the spine or in the hip joints are strongly advised to practise this *asana*. This *asana* also cures pain and corrects disorders of the shoulder joints, neck, arms and the palms. Since it is an easy *asana*, arthritics in any condition and of any age can practise it.

For the general practitioners, it is a good *asana* for creating flexibility in the spine, for removing wind and gastric troubles, and for correcting respiratory disorders.

SIDDHA ASANA

Persons with moderate joint pain of any type can be completely cured if they practise the *asanas* of the series already described above. The chronic cases, however, might take a little longer time for getting fully cured. Therefore, the arthritis patients with chronic trouble are advised to keep practising all the *asanas* of this series regularly. By continuing the practice they should be fully cured in two to three months.

It needs to be emphasized that one must take a proper diet along with the regular practice of yoga in order to get a satisfactory result. The diet for the arthritics has been fully described in the first part of this·chapter. It is expected that the arthritics take their meals according to those recommendations. I wish only to remind them not to take curd *(dahi)* bananas, and to avoid taking tea and cigarettes on empty stomach. With these clarifications, a new *asana* — *Siddha Asana* — is presented now. The method of practice and its benefits are described below:

Position of Readiness

Be seated on the carpeted floor. Stretch out both the legs in front. Keep your spine straight up and firm. Look in front. Keep the hands down on ·the floor. Breathe normally. This is the position of readiness.

Steps for Practice

(i) Fold the left leg back from the knee and bring the foot in front. Then stretch the toes and ankle of the left leg and try to bring them in a straight line. In case you find it difficult to bring them in a straight line, stretch them only as much as possible. Bring the heel near the testicles without pressing against them. Now your left knee should be on the floor. In case the knee cannot touch the floor, let it remain a little up and raised.

(ii) Now fold the right leg at the knee and bring the right foot on the top of the left foot. Keep the right heel just above the left heel. Then stretch the ankle of the right leg while keeping the right knee also on the floor. Keep the legs in the same condition. Do not put any pressure on the testicles.

(iii) Stretch out both the hands. Make a circular shape

with your thumb and the index finger in each hand. Then stretch out the remaining three fingers of each hand and keep them firmly together. Now put the right wrist on the right knee and the left wrist on the left knee. Make the arms and the hands tight. Keep the spine straight and firm. Fingers pointing downwards. Breathe normally. (Fig. 41).

(iv) Stay in this position for about one minute. After remaining in the same position for about one minute, loosen the fingers of both the hands. Then lift up the right leg by hand and put it down on the floor and stretch out the legs. After resting for a few seconds repeat once more by alternating the legs. This time your right foot will be underneath and the left foot will be on the top. Stay in this *asana* again for about a minute.

Daily Practice

Practise *Siddha Asana* for a maximum of three minutes only. Begin with about two minutes and gradually increase the time to three minutes daily. During this period you will be doing *Siddha Asana* only twice and the total time spent will be three minutes only. Do not practise it for more than three minutes in a single day.

Benefits

Siddha Asana has a curative effect on all the joints below the waist area. The hip joints, the knees and the ankles are very effectively activated during this *asana* and, as a result, the circulation of blood in these areas becomes normalised, the supply of synovial fluid (joint fluid) is restored, and the spasticity and pain are removed.

Siddha Asana has a good effect on the nervous system all over the body. People suffering from any kind of nerve defects will find this *asana* very beneficial. It is regarded as a vitally important *asana* for gaining the power of concentration and for acquiring mental equilibrium. Though it might appear a little difficult *asana* for the beginners, with regular practice, any person can do it properly.

111

NATRAJ ASANA

Position of Readiness

Stand up on the floor. Let the hands hang loosely on the sides. Make the body firm and straight. Look in front. Breathe normally. This is the position of readiness.

Steps for Practice

(i) Stand up on the left leg. Fold back the right leg at the knee. Grab all the toes of the right leg with the palm of the right hand. At this stage your right leg is just folded backwards and it is held by the palm. Keep the leg in the same position.

(ii) Then bring all the fingers of the left hand together and tighten the left hand. When the left hand has been tightened, slowly raise this hand up and at the same time slowly push the right leg backwards. In this process you are doing two things simultaneously. You are raising the left hand in front pushing the right foot backwards. While doing this, you should give a maximum backwards push with the right leg. But do not raise the left hand straight up towards the sky, keep it slanting, pointed towards the horizon, so that the whole hand is visible to you.

(iii) Now bend the body above the waist slightly forward and try to see the top of the finger of the left hand and keep looking there. Keep the right foot fully pushed back and tight. Make the left leg quite firm and tight. Do not loosen the left leg when you bend the body slightly forward. Stay in this position for about eight seconds, as shown in Fig. 42. Keep breathing normally, all through this *asana*. In case you have difficulty in doing this *asana* on the floor, stand with the support of either a wall or a pillar. After you have become used to practising it, do it standing on the floor, without any support.

(iv) After remaining in this position for about eight seconds, gradually bring the left hand tightly down and bring the right leg back to the folded position and then release it. You are now standing on both legs. Rest in that position for a while. After resting for a few seconds, repeat the *asana*. This time stand up on the right leg, hold the left leg and raise the right hand. You have to do it alternately by following the same process as during the first round.

Daily Practice

Make four rounds daily during the first week. During the second week and afterwards make six rounds daily. Practise it alternately. Do not make more than six rounds of *Natraj Asana* in a single day.

Benefits

Natraj Asana activates all the major and minor joints of the body in a single process. For the arthritics it has a great curative effect upon all the joints. It brings proper activation upon the shoulder joints, hip joints, the knees, the ankles, the palms and the fingers. Because of this conditioning, the muscles, nerves and tissues of these areas get normalized and their functioning is restored.

Natraj Asana has also a good effect upon the spine. It removes spinal rigidity and pain. It removes backache, stiffness, and other disorders of the spine.

To the general practitioners it provides flexibility to the limbs. Strengthens the major bones, enhances the digestive power, improves eyesight, and generates vitality, potency and the quality of determination. A significant aspect of *Natraj Asana* is that it symbolizes action. In other words, it breaks the condition of standstillness in the individual and creates a feeling to act. Because of these benefits, it is a highly recommended *asana* for the arthritics as well as for the general practitioners of yoga.

Proper Diet

A proper diet for the arthritic or rheumatic people means — to take what is beneficial and stop what is harmful. With this consideration, they are advised to stop taking the following things: bananas, and curd (yogurt). Those who smoke and take tabacco in any form, should stop it completely or should reduce its intake considerably. No more than two cups of coffee or tea should be taken within twenty-four hours.

They should eat four times daily. During breakfast they should eat an orange, apple or any fruit (except banana), germinated gram, *chapati* and green vegetables. They can take a cup of hot milk with ovaltine. The non-vegetarians can take boiled or poached egg. During lunch and dinner they should first take salad (a mixture of tomato, carrot, cucumber, radish, lettuce or any eatable raw vegetables such as, papaya and others). After eating about a cup of salad, they should eat wheat bread, green vegetables, *saag*, pulses (except *arhar* and *kesari*). The non-vegetarians can eat fish and liver with least amount of spices. They should avoid excessive use of hot spices, should drink ten to twelve glasses of fresh water, and should eat at least two hours prior to retiring time during night.

In the afternoon, they should take some light refreshment, such as some fresh fruits, salted biscuits, *chana ghughani* or *halwa* or cake or other similar items.

Hygienic Care

The most important thing about hygienic care is to bathe regular, keep the whole body clean and take proper care of teeth. Bath can be taken with hot or cold water as desired. The whole body should be thoroughly rubbed with a rough towel by applying some bathing soap. In order to have full benefit of water, rubbing of the whole body is essential.

It is also important to wear a clean undershirt *(ganji)*, underwear and other clothes. Neatness and cleanliness should be maintained in every day life as much as possible.

If the arthritics follow the above mentioned system of yoga therapy they should feel assured of getting fully cured from this disease. They are advised to begin their practice according to the method described in this chapter. During the first week they should practise only two to four *asanas* of this series. During the second week and after they should gradually add other *asanas*. They should never try to do all the *asanas* of this series during the first week.

6

Obesity

OBESITY IS becoming a common health hazard. Millions of people, male and female of every age, are carrying excessive extra weight on their bodies which they should not carry. The most frightening aspect of obesity is that it shortens the life span, causes atherosclerosis, coronary heart troubles, hypertension (high blood pressure), various physical-mental (psychosomatic) ailments and disorders, and makes the life of the person miserable due to development of such complications as diabetes, indigestion, gastrointestinal disorders, sexual incapacitation, and inferiority complex. Let me explain in detail what it is, what are the causing factors, and how it is corrected through Yogic methods.

For a better understanding of the problems related to obesity, we have to differentiate it from overweight. Overweight is not obesity. But every obese person is overweight. Overweight means carrying only a few pounds of extra weight than the bodyframe requires. In case of overweight, though there is unwanted and extra weight, it may not be quite excessive. For example, if a grown-up person of average height carries five to ten pounds of extra weight, he is overweight but not obese.

Unlike the overweight, the obese person's weight becomes almost static. Any grown-up person of average height carrying more than ten pounds of extra weight for years together is an obese person. The excessive weight begins to strain all the bodily organs of the obese constantly and as a consequence he faces health hazards. The charts given overleaf show how much average weight men and women should have.

Though obesity causes the same disproportionate accumulation of fat in men and women, there is some variation in them. In women, fat generally accumulates in the hip area and in the thighs. In men accumulation is mostly in the abdominal area and less so in other areas. But in course of time, in chronic cases of obesity this accumulation of fat and muscle covers the whole body. The fat then is not only localised but found all over the body.

Causes of Obesity

Though it is difficult to pinpoint the exact cause of obesity, it can fairly be stated that it is a consequence of excessive eating. It is true that other factors are also involved in it, but one thing is certain that without excessive eating generally there will not be obesity.

In treating the patients of obesity at the Indian Institute of Yoga, Patna, and also at the Yoga Institute of Washington, D.C., U.S.A., I have found that all obese people develop certain common habits, make some common errors, and they all have the following common characteristics.[1]

[1]The author founded the Yoga Institute of Washington in 1964 and taught Yoga to more than 8000 men and women till 1968. He had the opportunity to treat about 200 cases of obesity during his five years of yoga teaching.

The Indian Institute of Yoga, Patna, was founded in 1969 by the author and here also he has treated more than a hundred cases of obesity. The above observations are based on the findings of treatment of obese persons.

Average Weight for Men

Weight[*] in Lbs. according to age

Feet Inches	15-19 yrs	20-24 yrs	25-29 yrs	30-34 yrs	35-39 yrs	40-44 yrs	45-49 yrs	50-54 yrs	55-59 yrs
5-0	113	119	124	127	129	132	134	135	136
5-1	115	121	126	129	131	134	136	137	138
5-2	118	124	128	131	133	136	138	139	140
5-3	121	127	131	134	136	139	141	142	143
5-4	124	131	134	137	140	142	144	145	146
5-5	128	135	138	141	144	146	148	149	150
5-6	132	139	142	145	148	150	152	153	154
5-7	136	142	146	149	152	154	156	157	158
5-8	140	146	150	154	157	159	161	162	163
5-9	144	150	154	158	162	164	166	167	168
5-10	148	154	158	163	167	169	171	172	173
5-11	153	158	163	168	172	175	177	178	179
6-0	158	163	169	174	178	181	183	184	185
6-1	163	168	175	180	184	187	190	191	192
6-2	168	173	181	186	191	194	197	198	199

*Weight without wearing shoes and heavy clothes.

1 Kilo = 2.205 Lbs.

(i) They are addicted to overeating.

(ii) They eat most of the time.

(iii) All of them, without exception, eat faster without chewing the food properly.

(iv) They retire soon after dinner.

Average Weight for Women

Weight* in Lbs. according to age

Feet Inches	15-19 yrs	20-24 yrs	25-29 yrs	30-34 yrs	35-39 yrs	40-44 yrs	45-49 yrs	50-54 yrs	55-59 yrs
5-0	108	115	118	121	124	128	131	133	134
5-1	110	117	120	123	126	130	133	135	137
5-2	113	120	122	125	129	133	136	138	140
5-3	116	123	125	128	132	136	139	141	143
5-4	119	126	129	132	136	139	142	144	146
5-5	122	129	132	136	140	143	146	148	150
5-6	126	133	136	140	144	147	151	152	153
5-7	130	137	140	144	148	151	155	157	158
5-8	134	141	144	148	152	155	159	162	163
5-9	138	145	148	152	156	159	163	166	167
5-10	142	149	152	155	159	162	166	170	173
5-11	147	153	155	158	162	166	170	174	177
6-0	150	157	159	162	165	169	173	177	182

*Weight without wearing shoes and heavy clothes.

(v) They either purposely avoid or do not get time to do physical labour and exercises.

We can say that obesity, as it prevails nowadays, is the result of modern civilisation. All classes of people in the developed nations and the people of upper class in the developing nations are getting now more and better food and in many varieties than it was possible centuries ago. Moreover, the scientific developments and modern

118

facilities have made the life of the upper strata of the society so comfortable that they have hardly any need to do physical labour for a living. In the absence of any physical work, on the one hand, and daily intake of highly rich food, on the other, is bound to add extra weight.

In order to have a clear picture of life pattern of a modern man of well developed society, let me sketch briefly how he passes his daily life. A typical man's routine goes like this: He gets up in the morning, has bed tea, shaves, washes up, dresses up, has a sumptuous breakfast, comes down in an elevator, gets into his car, rides to his office building, takes the elevator upstairs, sits in his chair for office work, goes downstairs in an elevator to a restaurant in the same building, has delicacies for lunch, comes back to his office and sits there again till the closing time, and then takes his car and returns home. At home during the evening, he watches television while drinking beer or some other drinks. Then he has dinner of choicest food and plenty of drinks. Without waiting for even an hour, he retires to bed and goes to sleep. Again, he repeats the same routine the next day, and the day next to that, and so on.

As can be noticed from the above life-pattern the individual did not have to move around and he did not need to do any physical labour. On the other hand, he kept feeding himself the fatty, nourishing and high-calory food, day and night. In such cases, the body gets more food than it needs for its balanced growth and up-keep. As a result, overweight has to develop and in most cases, it takes the form of obesity. When the individual passes his days as described above, he gets so much used to his routined life that he feels helpless and a victim of his own luxuries and comforts. Many become addicted to certain types of food and habits and they need treatment for restoration of normal health as any other patient of chronic disease would need..

Another disheartening problem related to obesity is that the individual develops a feeling of inferiority. He does not like to meet his friends and the social groups. He begins to isolate himself and gets used to living a secluded

119

life. In isolation or in company of his own type; he prefers to eat something most of the time and develops certain bad habits, such as, taking alcoholic drinks, using intoxicating drugs and adopting various other harmful ways of living. The individual so isolated develops various types of mental disorders, such as, nervousness, tension, anxiety, fear, lack of confidence, etc. Thus, he entraps himself in a sort of a vicious circle. When he is nervous and in anxiety, he eats to pacify himself. And eating ultimately brings him back to the same mental condition he was already suffering from. Ultimately he develops various undesirable habits of living and it becomes difficult to restore him to normal health.

Yogic Treatment

The yogic method of correcting obesity primarily involves two things: (i) taking a balanced and proper diet, and (ii) practising a few selected *asanas*. Before describing both these aspects, a few pertinent observations need to be made.

In treating the obese persons at the Indian Institute of Yoga, Patna, and at the Yoga Institute of Washington, I have found that according to our process the average rate of reduction in weight is 1 to 1½ pounds per week. An obese person loses about 4 to 6 pounds of weight per month. Depending upon his total extra weight, the correction period for an obese person lasts for some months. For example, if a person carries 42 pounds of extra weight, the correcting period might continue for seven to ten months.

The biggest advantage of this yogic system of treatment is that the individual does not have to go on fasting and he does not feel any weakness. The reduction in weight is so gradual that the person does not feel any loss of strength. Due to gradual reduction, there is no sagging of the facial tissues or of the bodily skin and muscle. In this process, reduction of weight and body conditioning occur simultaneously. As a result by the time the obese has been restored to normal weight, his body becomes proportionate.

It might be argued that the yogic system takes too much time in correcting the excessive weight, whereas several manufacturers and advertisers of weight-reducing gadgets, food packages, pills and drugs claim to reduce weight in a matter of days and weeks. Such advertisements probably attract millions of people by their big claims for reducing weight. But these 'gimmicks' do not bring any lasting result and cause various ailments, disorders and even do serious physical-mental harm to the users. I have been shocked to see several young girls and boys in the U.S.A. and also in India ruining their health, beauty and mental balance by using these 'gimmicks' and 'quickies'.

Yogic method, though time-consuming, is preferable and desirable for several reasons. It reduces weight in a lasting and permanent way without causing any ill effect to health, beauty and physical/mental condition. It does not cost a penny to correct the disorder. There is no disturbance to normal life, nor is there any possibility of regaining the same weight even if yoga practice is discontinued and only the method of eating is maintained.

It is advised that once the weight has been reduced to normal level, the individual should keep practising yoga even for ten to fifteen minutes per day. In case yoga practice is stopped for some reasons, the individual should continue to follow the yogic principles and method of eating. By taking a proper and balanced diet, the normalcy in weight will always remain the same.

Selected Yoga Asanas

The overweight and the obese have to practise yoga on a selected basis. It would not be possible for them to perform all types of *asanas* at the initial stage. Nor is it necessary to practise some of the difficult *asanas* for the desired result. There are several *asanas* which are simple and easy to do, but have remarkable impact on weight reduction and body-conditioning. Therefore, the practitioners are advised to begin their practice according to the selection of *asanas* given below:

A word of advice — that you should not try to do too

many *asanas* in the beginning. Proceed gradually but regularly. Start with the *asanas* recommended for the first week and go on adding the *asanas* of the second, third and other weeks. This way your progress would be gradual, steady and without any strain and exhaustion. The result would begin to show right from the first week, even though you would be practising only a few yoga *asanas*. With these clarifications, now let me recommend what you need to practise during the first week and afterwards.

Yogic Treatment

During the first week, start with the following *asanas:*

1. *Ekpada Uttan Asana:* Described in Chapter 4. Make a total of eight rounds — four rounds with each leg alternately.

2. *Uttanpada Asana:* Described in Chapter 2. Make a total of only four rounds daily. Never practise it more than six rounds in a day.

Rest

After practising both the *asanas* noted above, rest in *Shava Asana* for a period of five minutes. See Chapter 2 for the method of practising *Shava Asana.*

Second Week

Keep practising both the *asanas* of the first week and the following *asanas:*

3. *Bhujanga Asana:* Described in Chapter 2. Practise four rounds daily.

4. *Shalabha Asana:* Described in Chapter 2. Practise four rounds daily.

After practising all the four *asanas*, rest in *Shava Asana* for five minutes.

Third Week

Keep practising all the four *asanas* of the preceding weeks and add the following *asanas* at the start of third week:

5. *Santulan Asana:* (Described in Chapter 5) Make a

Fig 27   Simha Asana

Fig 28 Half Sarvanga Asana

Fig 29   Sarvanga Asana

Fig 30   Matsya Asana with Lotus Pose

Fig 31   Easy Matsya Asana

Fig 32   Santulan Asana

Fig 33   First Phase of Trikona Asana

Fig 34 Second Phase of Trikona Asana

Fig 35 Third Phase of Trikona Asana

Fig 36 Final Phase of Trikona Asana

total of six rounds daily—practise three rounds with each side, alternately.

6. *Pawanmukta Asana:* (Described in Chapter 2) Make a total of six rounds daily—practise three rounds with each side, alternately.

After practising all the six *asanas*, rest in *Shava Asana* for a period of seven minutes.

Fourth Week

Keep practising all the six *asanas* of the preceding weeks and add the following *asanas* at the beginning of fourth week:

7. *Suryanamaskar Asana:* (Described in Chapter 3) make four rounds daily.

8. *Dhanur Asana:* (Described in Chapter 3) Make four rounds daily.

After practising all the eight *asanas*, rest in *Shava Asana* for a period of ten minutes.

Fifth Week

Keep practising all the eigh *asanas* of the preceding weeks and add the following *asanas* at the beginning of fifth week:

9. *Ardha Vakra Asana:* (Described in Chapter 3) Make only four rounds daily—two rounds with each side.

10. *Paschimottan Asana:* (Described in Chapter 2) Make only four rounds daily.

After practising all the *asanas*, rest now for ten minutes in *Shava Asana.*

Sixth Week and Onwards

Add the following *asanas* during the sixth week and in your onward practice:

11. *Supta Vajra Asana:* (Described in Chapter 3) Make only four rounds daily.

12. *Matsyendra Asana:* (Described in Chapter 3) Make only four rounds—two rounds with each side.

MANDUKA ASANA

Position of Readiness

For doing this *asana*, you need a padded floor. Therefore, put a blanket or folded ·cloth on the floor. Be seated on your folded legs, as shown in Fig. 15. You should be in the same position as you have to be in the sitting position for making *Suptavajra Asana*. Being seated in this position, breathe normally. This is the position of readiness.

Steps for Practice

(i) By giving more body weight on the right foot lessen the weight on the left foot. This will make it possible for you to push the left foot out to the left side of the hip.

(ii) Then by putting body weight on the left side, release the right foot and push it out to the right side of the hip. Now you are sitting on the floor and your left foot is folded on the left side and the right foot is folded on the right side. Keep the palms on the floor to support the body weight. In case this is painful, do not proceed further, practise with this for some time. When you have no difficulty in reaching this stage, proceed on with the following steps:

(iii) While keeping hands on the floor on both sides and partially supporting the body weight, separate the knees gradually. Move the left knee further to the left side and the right knee to the right side. Try to separate them as much as you can do so comfortably.

(iv) When the knees have been separated to a feasible point, stay there and do the following: Bring the palms on the knees on their respective sides. Make the body straight. Look in front. Breathe normally, Stay in this position for eight to twelve seconds. You should be as shown in Fig. 43.

(v) After staying in that position for the desired time, return to the sitting position by the following method: Put your palms on the floor and make a kneeling position. Then bring forward any foot in front first by sliding it under the hip area. Now bring the other leg also in front. Then sit comfortably and relax. After resting for six to eight seconds, repeat this *asana* a few times more by following the same process.

132

Daily Practice

Do it twice daily during the first week. Gradually develop the practice to a maximum of four times daily.

Benefits

It is very effective *asana* reducing weight of the thighs, hip and the abdominal areas. For ladies and gents both, it has good conditioning impact on the muscles and nerves of the lower areas of the body.

This *asana* has several other benefits. It activises all the joints of the lower area of the body, enhances sexual potentiality, corrects disorders of the reproductive system, cures piles, and strengthens the digestive system. With a little effort this *asana* can be practised by any person.

Proper Diet

Breakfast (7 to 9 A.M.)

(i) Fruit juice—one cup of juice of any fruit, such as, orange, apple or pineapple.

(ii) Fresh fruits—one apple, or one guava, or one banana, or two peaches.

(iii) Germinated gram (chickpeas) — 1/4 cup

(iv) Wheat bread or toast—two pieces
or
cornflakes, or oatmeal, or wheat *dalia* with milk and sugar

(v) Eggs (if desired)—one (boiled, poached or scrambled)

(vi) Tea or coffee—one cup (if desired)

Lunch and Dinner (12 to 2 P.M., 6 to 8 P.M.)

(i) Salad (a mixture of tomato, cucumber, radish lettuce, carrot, etc., with salt, pepper and lemon juice or with salad dressing)—about one cup

(ii) Soup of any type—one cup

(iii) Rice, bread or *chapati*

(iv) Leafy vegetables (*saag*) of any kind

(v) Green vegetables of any kind

(vi) Pulse (*moong, masur, chana* or any kind)

Note: The non-vegetarians can take fish or liver or any sea-food, but should avoid taking meat and chicken for a few months, if possible. Such restrictions on diet·would help in solving the problem of obesity.

Afternoon Refreshment (3 to 5 P.M.)

(i)   Fresh fruit of any kind—one or two pieces

(ii)   Salted biscuits—a few pieces
    or
    Chana ghughani—about a cup
    or
    Dry fruits (a mixture of cashew, almond, pecan, pistachio and walnut)—¼ cup

(iii)   Tea or coffee—one cup (if needed)

The above mentioned diet chart provides just an outline of items to be taken for breakfast, lunch, afternoon refreshment and dinner. The chart does not explain the method, principles and essential requirements. Without observance of these vitally important aspects, just eating according to the diet chart would not bring a satisfactory result. The chart becomes meaningful and important when the following principles, method and requirements are observed sincerely.

Principles and Requirements of Eating

(i)   The first and most important principle is to eat slowly after chewing and crushing the food quite thoroughly.

(ii)   The second vitally imporant principle is to finish eating (specially dinner) at least two hours prior to sleeping time during night.

(iii)   The third and the most important principle is: *Never eat more than 85 per cent* of your capacity at any time. In other words, *always eat a little less than you need.*

(iv)   Avoid drinking water while eating. Drink water after half an hour of eating. Take ten to fifteen glasses of fresh water in twenty-four hours.

(v)   Do not eat fatty, fried and highly seasoned food.

Avoid hot spices, pickles, *chutney* and sweets. Prepare your dishes by using the least amount of spices for flavour.

(vi) Eat only four times in twenty-four hours, that is, take breakfast in the morning, lunch at noon, some light refreshment in the afternoon, and dinner at night. Avoid eating any thing in between these four fixed hours.

By following the principles and method of eating as described above and by practising yoga *asanas* as mentioned below, you can be sure of losing a minimum of six pounds of weight every month.

7

Mental Problems

MIND LOSES its equilibrium when any external or internal problem strains it harshly. Consequently, its functioning gets disturbed and its harmony begins to diminish, slowly or rapidly, depending upon the individual's state of mental health. The person so affected for a long period, becomes mentally sick with an intensity proportionte to the degree of harmony lost. As a result, the individual's thought, action, manner, behaviour and outlook become imbalanced, and take various forms and shapes of abnormal expressions. This can involve persons of any age, of any sex, of any socio-economic background and of any land. Here we are faced then, with two types of problems: (i) how to correct and cure the cases of mental sickness, and (ii) how and in what way one can maintain sound mental health? The answer to both-curative and preventive problems-we find in the system of yoga.

Cause of Mental Troubles

In order to make the methodological processes of Yoga comprehensible, a brief discussion about the causes of mental troubles is essential. All troubles which affect the mind of an individual spring from three basic sources: (i) Nature, (ii) Society, and (iii) Self. In other words, the particular problem which strains and causes mental imbalance in an individual is either nature-oriented, society-oriented or self-oriented which have been termed as *Davik*, *Bhautik* and *Atmik* by Kapil in his Samkhya philosophy.

The problems arising out of nature could be in the form of some natural calamity, danger from certain animate creatures, and the peculiarity of natural phenomena. The societal problems, likewise, could be religious, ethnic, racial, economic, political, etc., or also they might involve the varied problems of adjustment to certain customs, manners, ways of life, etc., of a particular community. Similarly, there could be countless problems of individual's own creation, which arise because of certain beliefs, faith, notions, habits, manners and also because of some inner feelings, such as, hatred, jealousy, revenge, love, romance, likes and dislikes.

People of every society, be that industrial, agrarian, tribal or primitive, have been faced with various problems arising out of these three above mentioned sources, more or less, in the same way as we have to face them today. Though the nature and forms of human problems have changed because of changes in social conditions, yet basically, they remain the same. Seen in this context, it would be interesting to know what the early thinkers of yoga have thought over these human problems and what solutions they have provided.

Among the forefathers whose contribution became the foundation of yoga system is that of Kapil. Therefore, let us first see what Kapil had to say on this problem.

The contribution of Kapil (700 B.C.) is called Samkhya philosophy.[1] According to Kapil, the answer to all human problem is in *samyak jnana*, (proper knowledge). In the absence of *samyak jnana*, the unfamiliar and peculiar

---

[1] The most authentic book of Samkhya philosophy available is by Ishwar Krishna, *Samkhya Karika* (Delhi: Motilal Banarsi Das), 1966.

happenings cause *dukha* (sorrow). When the individual develops and acquires proper knowledge about *Purusha* (self) and *Prakriti* (Nature), then the peculiar happenings and causations in any of the three sources (mentioned above) do not cause *dukha*. This implies acquiring a scientific knowledge about *rajas, tamas* and *sattva gunas,* and all the *tattvas* (elements) of *Prakriti* together with a knowledge about the composition, function and co-relationship of sense, organs, action organs, mind, intelligence and the totality of the *Purusha* (self). When the individual becomes so knowledgeable, he attains the power of overcoming pain, maintains mental equilibrium and obtains pleasure, happiness and excellence in life.

But this Samkhya philosophy did not show the method and process of obtaining the goal. It needed a comprehensive system in order to help the individual adopt and achieve what had been so rightly stated by Kapil. This system was propounded by Patanjali in his *Yoga Sutra.* Therefore, it is essential to understand what Patanjali had to say.

Patanjali's Yoga Sutra

The *Yoga Sutra* of Patanjali (300 B.C.) is a treatise on methodological process for obtaining the goal laid down by Kapil and adds something more. Whereas Kapil emphasized acquiring of *jnana* which involves only the mind, Patanjali's system of yoga, on the other hand, involves both mind and body. In this respect, the *Purusha* of Patanjali has to do two things simultaneously, that is, he must acquire *samyak jnana* and also he must practise yoga in order to achieve excellence of both body and mind. This way, by combining 'jnana and practices' together the individual would attain not only excellent health but would also be able to maintain a harmonious relationship between the mind and the body. Thus, we find that Patanjali's yoga provides a better and more thorough answer to our problems of mental health than what is provided by Kapil.

Since Patanjali's system involves knowing and doing both, his method includes all those steps which are essential for obtaining the desired goal on both levels-physical and mental. These steps are eight in number. They are mentioned below together with their basic meanings and implications:

Yama (control and discipline) *Niyama* (rules, methods and principles), *Asanas* (making body postures) *Pranayama (kriyas* with air), *Pratyahara* (avoidance of undesirables in taking actions, that is, knowing the proper actions), *Dharana* (concentration), *Dhyana* (meditation), and *Samadhi* (contemplation).

Since these eight steps of Patanjali were not very comprehensively discussed in his *Yoga Sutra,* further works were necessary for covering them properly. In order to facilitate the practitioners, these steps were later grouped under different yogas according to their nature and substance. The yogas which cover all these steps are the following four:

JNANA YOGA

Covers *Yama* and *Niyama and is the science of acquiring proper knowledge.*

HATHA YOGA

Covers *Asanas* and *Pranayamas* and is the science of physical excellence.

KARMA YOGA

Covers *Pratyahra* and is the science of action.

RAJA YOGA

Covers *Dharana, Dhyana* and *Samadhi* and is the science of concentration and meditation.

Applied Yoga

It needs to be clearly stated that not all types of mental cases can be helped through yoga. This limitation becomes imperative because it is assumed that those going to practise yoga have the mental capability to understand its basic principles, methods and thoughts and are physically in a condition to perform even the simplest practices. Unless these basic requirements about the physical and mental status are fulfilled, it would be difficult for persons concerned to make proper use of yoga. With this understanding, the process of treatment and steps are described here. These recommendations are based on our experiences in correcting and curing various cases of mental illness at the Indian Institute of Yoga, Patna.

Jnana and Karma Yogas

Persons suffering from mental disorders are advised to know the basic tenets of Jnana Yoga and Karma Yoga. Both these yogas relate to the essentials of *samyak jnana* (acquiring of proper knowledge) and of *satkaryavad* (science of action). These yogas involve knowing certain basic concepts, theories, principles and thoughts concerning the Self, Society and Nature. A knowledge of these would equip the individual to understand the causations and happenings in a given situation and would make him knowledgeable to act properly for obtaining a satisfactory result. This being the importance of these two yogas,[1] the individual should know them along with the practices of Hatha Yoga.

Guidelines

In order to achieve the full benefits of yoga it is important that the practitioners have a proper understanding of the essentials of yoga practice. These essentials have been briefly described in Chapter 1. People with mental problems are advised to read the first chapter with special attention to: (a) therapeutic yoga, (b) essentials of yoga practice, (c) proper diet, and (d) bathing and cleaning. A proper understanding of these above

---

[1]For a proper understanding of these yogas, please read Swami Vivekananda. *The Yoga and Other Works* (New York: Ramakrishna-Vivekananda Centre, 1955). Both *Jnana Yoga* and *Karma Yoga* are included in this single edition. These books are now available in Hindi and other languages in India, published by Ramkrishna Mission.

mentioned aspects and their adoption would provide a very satisfactory result to the practitioners.

With the knowledge of the first chapter, they should begin practising Hatha Yoga according to the stages and steps outlined below:

Hatha Yoga

Hatha Yoga is comprised of *Pranayamas, asanas, bandhas* and *mudras*. People with mental problems are advised to practise only some of the selected items in the initial stage. When the normal mental condition is restored, they could try other items of Hatha Yoga according to their own liking and preference. With this understanding, they are recommended to begin their practice on the following basis:

Yogic Treatment
First Week

It should begin with the practice of *Ujjayee Pranayama* in 'lying position'. It is easy to do and any person can practise it. The method of practising *Ujjayee* in 'lying position' is fully described in Chapter 4. They should practise only five rounds of it daily.

After making five rounds of *Ujjayee*, they should practise *Suryanamaskar Asana* and *Uttanpada Asana*. Four rounds of each of the above two *asanas* would be sufficient. Do not make more than four rounds of each. Follow the method of doing *Suryanamaskar* as given in Chapter 3 and that of *Uttanpada* as given in Chapter 2.

When all the three above mentioned items have been practised, the practitioner should rest either in *Shava Asana* or by just lying on the back with normal breathing. This rest should be for five minutes at the end of all the three items.

Second and Third Week

During the second week they should add the following *asanas:*

Paschimottan Asana: Described in Chapter 2
Bhujanga Asana: Described in Chapter 2

141

Trikona Asana: Described in Chapter 5

After practising all the *asanas* and the *Pranayama* mentioned above, they should now rest in *Shava Asana* (as described in Chapter 2) for ten to fifteen minutes.

Fourth Week

During the fourth week they should gradually add either all the *asanas* given below or they should choose and practise only those which they can perform comfortably:

Sarvanga Asana: Described in Chapter 4

Matsya Asana: Described in Chapter 4

Dhanur Asana: Described in Chapter 3

Hala Asana: Described below.

HALA ASANA

This *asana* is one of the best *asana* of Hatha Yoga system. It has some unique qualities and excellent benefits. Due to these, it occupies a very prominent place in the list of *asanas*.

This *asana* can be performed in two ways. Though one form is easier than the other; both have almost the same effects and rewards. Since it is a valuable *asana*, the methodological process of both forms is described and explained separately. Let me present the easier one first.

Form 1
Position of Readiness

Lie flat on the back. Stretch out the whole body. Make yourself quite straight. Bring the heels together and the toes together. Put the palms on the floor and keep them quite close to the body on both sides. Make your neck and head straight. You should be as in the readiness position of *Uttanpada Asana.* You are now ready for the actual performance.

Steps for Practice

First stretch out the legs and make them tight. Let the toes be also stretched and pointing in opposite direction to the head. Now inhale and simultaneously raise both legs upward, till they come to a vertical position. Synchronize inhaling and lifting of the legs. Keep both palms on the floor where they were.

Second, when you have reached the vertical point, start exhaling and simultaneously start lowering the legs towards the head area. Try to touch the floor in front of the head, at a distance the toes can possibly touch. Go only as far as is possible for you. Stay at the point where you can and stabilize yourself there. After the exhaling is over, keep breathing normally till the whole posture is completed. You should now be as shown in Fig. 44. Remain in this position for about eight to ten seconds. You are now in the Plough Pose.

Note : As long as you are in second phase, keep the legs quite tight. Do not bend the legs at the knees. Keep the toes stretched and pointing or touching the ground. Keep both palms on the floor and the arms and hands straight and quite firm.

Third, after remaining in the econd phase for about ten seconds, start returning the back to the floor. Control this returning phase. Let the back roll down on the floor, inch by inch. It is very important that you return gradually, slowly and smoothly. Keep the legs and toes quite tight all along during the returning phase. Legs should be like a stick. When the heels touch the ground, let the whole body relax. You have completed one round of the famous Plough posture. Now relax for six to eight seconds. Then try some more rounds in the same manner as the first one.

Limitation

Begin with two rounds. Develop it to a maximum of four rounds. A regular practice of two or three rounds would be quite satisfactory.

Form 2
Position of Readiness

The position of readiness for Form 2 is same as for the

Form 1. Therefore, make yourself ready according to the directions given there.

Steps for Practice

First, inhale and raise both hands upwards in a parallel way, like two sticks. Bring the hands in front of the head and put the back of palms on the floor, parallel to each other. You should synchronize your inhaling and lifting of the hands in such a way that up to the time the hands have touched the floor you have continued inhaling. When the hands touch the floor, exhale.

Second, soon after this exhaling is over, start inhaling and at the same time start lifting both the legs upwards. Now, while inhaling, bring both legs up to a vertical position.

When the legs have reached the vertical point, start exhaling and at the same time start, lowering the legs towards the floor in front of the head, and above the fingers. Now put your toes on the floor. If you cannot touch the floor with the toes, go only as far down as is possible for you. After this last exhaling is over, keep breathing normally. Do not hold the breath. Make efforts for breathing normally. Stabilise yourself at the point, wherever you can.

At this point, pay attention to a few things: Your legs should remain quite tight, like sticks. The toes should be stretched out and on the floor or nearer to the floor side. Do not slacken or bend the knees. Try to keep the arms, hands and palms parallel to one another. With these requirements fulfilled, you are in perfect Plough Posture as shown in Fig. 45. Be in this phase for about ten seconds.

Third, after being in the Plough Pose for about ten seconds, return gradually and in a controlled way according to the following method. This returning process has the same importance as making the whole posture. Therefore pay all the attention for a smooth, slow and controlled return. Let the shoulders roll back first, then the flanks, then the small of the back, then the hip and lastly, the thighs, the legs and the heels in that order. Try to roll back inch by inch.

While returning, keep the hands on the floor, where they are. Withdraw only the legs. Roll back the whole body and let the heels fall on the floor. When the heels have touched the floor, lift both hands up and return them in a parallel way, like two parallel sticks, to the floor. Now put the palms on the floor. You have completed one round of the best form of Plough Posture. Now relax. Let the whole body be loose. Relax for about six to eight seconds. Then make a few more rounds in the same order as the first one.

Limitation

Make one round on the first day. Gradually go to four rounds in a few days. Four rounds are the maximum.

Benefits

The Plough Posture has some special values. According to Tantrik Yoga, it is the unique *asana* for gaining sexual powers. It invigorates, energizes and nourishes all the sexual glands and brings power, strength and vitality to all of them. Further, it has curative and corrective values for any weakened condition of the sex-glands. Due to these values, it has a medicinal effect in case of impotency, frigidity and lack of sexual power.

There are several other excellent benefits of this *asana*. It exercises every inch of the backbone. The whole spinal cord is normalized and soothened. Thus, so far as the flexibility of the spine is concerned, it surpasses all other *asanas* in effect.

The Plough Posture has excellent effect on correcting the extra weight. It reduces the excess weight without weakening the body. It makes the body proportionate by reducing the waistline, by toning up the digestive system, by taking off the fat, and by activating the whole nerve system.

It has a very good effect on the facial area also. Since there is a speedy circulation of the blood and since there is centralization of the same in the upper regions, the Plough Posture nourishes the whole area and thereby increases and restores the youthful look of the face, besides activations.

After practising the above mentioned *asanas* the practitioner should rest for ten to fifteen minutes in *Shava Asana*. When the practice of *Pranayama* and *asanas* have been regularized for about a month they should add the practice of concentration as described below.

RAJA YOGA : CONCENTRATION

Concentration is the primary step of Raja Yoga. Its next advanced stage is meditation. Before describing the method of practising concentration let me mention briefly what it is and what it does.[2]

Concentration means one-pointedness of the mind according to the will of the individual. By acquiring this power, the individual becomes master of his own mind and controls its fluctuations. His mind is not allowed the freedom to fly out and attach itself with countless issues, events, thoughts and objects. The involvement of the mind becomes selective and for some desirable purpose. Meaningless and worthless attachment is cut out. When this power of concentration is achieved through proper training, it has a great curative effect over the condition of mental sickness. This curative effect of concentration can be understood better when the nature of mind and also the mind-body relationship are explained.

Mind, by its nature, always tries to associate itself with some issues, events, objects or thoughts. Its involement is with only one thing at a time, though the duration may be for a shorter or longer period. To what it will attach itself with, is unpredictable.

The associative nature of the mind creates one specific condition in the body, which must be understood. As in the nature of the objects, issues or events with which the mind attaches itself, so it generates a likewise raction in the body. In other words, the nature of reaction is the same

---

[2]For more on concentration see: Dr. Phulgenda Sinha, *Yoga: Meaning, Values and Practice* (Bombay: Jaico Publishing House, 1972), pp. 15–32.

as is the nature of the object of involvement. Accordingly, when the mind attaches with something which by its nature could arouse anger in the individual, then it will generate in his body all those conditions and changes which anger does arouse by its very nature. The uncalled for attachment of the mind, by its nature, would arouse uncalled for conditioing of his bodily system resulting at times into tension, excitement and temper and at others, into pleasure and thrill. It is strongly held in yoga that unless distraction of the mind is controlled and its energy is properly channelled towards the desired purpose, nothing worth naming can be accomplished by the individual. This ability to control the mind and to channel it in the chosen direction is achieved through the training in concentration. For practising concentration, you have to make certain preparations as described below:

Arranging the Object

Place a vase with flower on some household furniture of small height so that the top of the flower remains in level with your eyes in the sitting position. You can put either a bunch of flowers or a single big one in the vase. The flower can be either natural or artificial. Keep the flower at about five feet in front of your sitting place. There should be a distance of about five feet between the object and the practitioner.

Method of Practising Concentration

When the flowers are arranged properly, be seated in an easy pose as shown in Fig. 46. For making this easy pose, you have to fold both the legs at the knees and put the body weight on the floor. After being in easy pose, first bring the left hand on the lap and put the right hand on the palm of the left hand. This will make your right palm facing upwards on the top of the left palm.

Then make the body straight. Your head, neck and the spine should be in one line and straight up. After the body has been straightened up, do not tighten it. Rather, let the body be relaxed while keeping it firm in straight-up position. Breathe normally. You are now in *Sukha Asana* (easy pose) as shown in Fig. 46. and ready to begin the practice of *dharana* (concentration), the first step of controlling the fluctuations of the mind. Follow the steps suggested below:

Now look at the flower petals. Keep looking for about ten seconds. In case you feel any pain in the eyes, look for a shorter time. But try not to blink the eyes. When you have looked at the flower for ten seconds, then close your eyes gently and try to see the shape of the flower in your mind. Keep your eyes closed for about ten seconds, while you are trying to recall the image and shape of the flower in your mind. After keeping the eyes closed for ten seconds, open them and again look at the flower for ten seconds. Repeat this process of seeing closing and seeing. That is, seeing through the eyes, closing the eyes and then seeing through the inner eye. Repeat this process only five times in one session during the first week. Gradually develop it upto ten and then upto fifteen times, which should remain as the limit. Here, time means round. Ten times would mean ten rounds. If you practise ten rounds only in one session that will be quite sufficient. But, in no case go beyond fifteen rounds in a single session.

When the practice is over, keep sitting still. Now loosen the body and sit in a relaxed way for two minutes. When you have done this, your practice in concentration is complete and over. After the session is over, you are free to eat, sleep or do any other work.

Some Suggestions

It is suggested that after practising with a single flower for about a month, if you like, you may add more flowers in the vase, though this additon of flowers is not necessary.

It is also suggested that after two months of practise with flowers, you could change the object. You could then practise with some photo, statue or painting of your own liking. The only consideration which you should have is about the size, colour and kind. They should be of medium size, of bright colour and of soothing, pleasing but never of thrilling kind.

Caution

The practitioners of concentration must read the following warnings and always keep them in mind while practising. As in any other science, the rules of Raja Yoga should also be cautiously followed in order to avoid undesirable consequences. Thus, the following warnings:

The first warning is about the limitation of time. The total time devoted to this practice of concentration should not exceed more than ten to fifteen minutes. Unless the teacher is personally guiding the practice, the practitioners should keep the whole practice of concentration within the limit of ten to fifteen minutes only within a period of twenty four hours.

The limitation is necessary for good reasons. One is that some practitioners migh` be fascinated by the peculiar imges flashing up before the inner eye while being in the process of practice. This fascination, unless checked, might mislead the practitioner into misusing his time. Second, if the practitioner keeps practising for getting thrills and fascinations, then, he is not only diverting himself from the desired goal, but also taking himself to some unknown consequence which might ill-affect his actions, thoughts, performances and behaviour. A limit of time, therefore, will always keep the practitioners within the safe side of practice where no undesirable consequence would ever be felt and known.

Testing Concentration

Whether you have gained concentration or not, you can test yourself, according to the following guidelines. While practising, when you do not see anything through the inner eye, you have not gained concentration. While practising, when you see some other objects through your inner eye but not the one placed before your outer eyes, you are improving but still have not gained concentration. But while practising, when you see the shape of the actual object through the inner eye even for a second, you have gained concentration. When the object remains before the inner eye, in any form and shape, for upto five seconds you

149

have gained good concentration. When you can hold the same shape or image for upto ten seconds, you have gained a very high level of concentration. And when you have gained concentration, your mental sickness or disorders are gone and you are fully restored to normal life.

8

Neck And Spinal Pain

SINCE BOTH these pains are related to spine, they have been covered under this chapter together. Readers will have no difficulty in following them, as they are distinctly described one by one. First we will discuss the Neck pain.

NECK PAIN

In medical terminology, neck pain affecting the cervical spine is called Cervical Spondylosis. This pain could be spread over to both sides of shoulders, the back side of the neck, the collar-bone and the shoulder joints. In certain cases, the pain might be in both the arms and also in the arms joints.

In medical system of treatment the patients are given medicines, heat compression and a collar on the neck. Though these medicinal aids provide some relief to the patients, they do not guarantee complete cure. Being uncertain of their medicinal effect, it is not uncommon for the medical man to advise their patients also to do some physical exercises for curing it. From our experience it has been found that such physical exercises are less effective compared to yoga postures. This is evident from the fact that whereas there is uncertainty of cure through physical exercise and medicines there is certainty of complete cure through yoga without any medicines. Before describing the yogic method of treatment, let me explain briefly the cause and cure of this ailment.

Cause and Cure

The causes of neck pain can be several. It could be due to regular use of a very high pillow under the head while sleeping. Another reason could be keeping the head bent in a particular posture for long hours intead of keeping it erect. It could also be due to rigidity of the muscles and nerves in the neck and shoulder areas which obstruct the proper circulation of blood.

Yogic method of treatment implies (i) taking proper diet; (ii) correcting the errors and faulty habits; and (iii) practising some selected yoga asanas. Diet for the patients of neck pain is the same as recommended to Arthritic patients in Chapter 5. The patients should take their diet as recommended therein. In order to obtain the full benefits of yoga, the patients are also advised to read Chapter 1 for acquiring an understanding of the yogic method of treatment and about the essential requirements of its practice.

The patient should use a thin pillow while sleeping and should avoid excessive bending of the neck. The rigidity of the muscles and the condition of defective circulation of blood will be automatically corrected through the practice of yoga.

Yogic Treatment

Practice of the following asanas is advised. During the first week, practise only the *Vriksha Asana*, *Trikona Asana* and *Bhujanga Asana*. After the completion of these three *Asanas*, *Shava Asana* should be practised for three minutes.

From the second week onwards, practise all the asanas in the order they are listed below. After practising all the six *asanas* of this selection, do the *Shava Asana* for five to seven minutes.

Asanas to cure the Neck Pain

Vriksha Asana: Described in Chapter 5
Trikona Asana: Described in Chapter 5
Bhujanga Asana: Described in Chapter 2
Gomukha Asana: Described in Chapter 5
Veera Asana: Described in Chapter 5
Jalandhar Bandha: Described below

JALANDHAR BANDHA

Position of Readiness

Sit down on the floor either in *Padma Asana* (Lotus pose) as shown in Fig. 1 or in *Sukha Asana* (Easy pose) as shown in Fig. 2 in Chapter 2. Hold the spine, neck and head absolutely erect and in one line. Look forward straight at the level of your eyes. Place your palms on their respective side of knees for making *Jalandhar Bandha* as shown in Fig. 47. Breath normally. You are now ready for making the *Jalandhar Bandha*. Follow the steps as described below:

Steps for Practice

(i)   Inhale 'slowly taking as much air as you can comfortably.

(ii) Hold the breath and bend your head downwards slowly, in such a way that the chin touches the chest. While bending your head do not strain yourself. If the chin does not touch the chest, go down as low as you can and stay there.

(iii) After the chin has touched the chest or is near to it, raise both the shoulders a little upwards. Keep your spine erect. Keep your head and neck straight while you hold the breath.

(vi) Stay in that position for 4 to 8 seconds while holding your breath inside. This makes the *Jalandhar Bandha* complete.

(v)   Now start raising your head upwards gradually. While the chin leaves the chest, start exhaling slowly. When the head is straight and you have exhaled, rest for two breaths. In other words, breathe in and breathe out without holding the air.

(vi)   After resting for two breaths, repeat this *Bandha* in the same process as done during the first round.

Daily Practice

Do four rounds daily. Start with three during the first week and then go upto four rounds from the second week onwards.

Benefits

This *Bandha* has medicinal value for curing the disorders of the head, shoulders and the cervical regions. It is also good for curing any disorder of the throat and face. People suffering from sinus and breathing trouble will find this *Bandha* very beneficial. It is easy to practice and can be performed by people of any age.

SPINAL PAIN

Spinal Pain here refers to disorders and pains in the spine, particularly in the waist region. This pain is commonly called the low-backache. This pain could be spread over to both sides of the waist and the hips. When the pain is acute, it makes the patient almost an invalid for making any free physical movement. In acute conditions, the patient is bed ridden.

It is generally found that people carrying extra weight develop spinal pain as they grow older. I have even found some young people suffering from this pain. The low-backache, at the initial stage might be tolerable and the individual might be able to bear it for some years. But prolonged pain of this type becomes chronic and gets aggravated at some later stages.

Causes and Cure

There are mainly four causes for this disorder; (i) faulty ways of eating resulting into overweight or underweight condition of the body; (ii) exposure to cold; (iii) physical straining of the spine; and (iv) a bad sitting posture for some considerable length of time.

It has been found that a large number of people suffering from spinal pain are in the habit of drinking water or tea or both after getting up in the morning. Some people first drink water and then take hot tea or coffee when they get up in the morning. This regular drinking of water and tea upon arising in the morning leads to forced elimination of the bowels, which in turn weakens the digestive system. The empty condition of the stomach affects the condition of the spine specially when the individual takes a bath or is exposed to the cold. The spinal region near the waist gets strained due to exposure and the person develops spinal pain. Excessive weight migh be another reason for straining the spine. It could also be due to some sudden physical strain or due to habitually defective ways of sitting.

We have found that the spinal pain is fully and permanently cured by yogic methods. It is only the restoration and correction period which varies. If the pain has been there for one year, it may take two months or even more to cure it fully. If the pain is les than one year, restoration period could be within four to five weeks.

The yogic method of treatment implies taking the correct diet, sleeping on not too soft a bed and practising some selected asanas. The diet for patients of spinal pain is the same as recommended to arthritic patients in Chapter 5. A special advice is to stop taking tea or water upon arising in the morning. It would be better if tea and coffee are completely stopped for a period of two months. The patients should not eat bananas and curd (*dahi*). They should avoid eating fatty, spicy and fried stuffs. For a better understanding of correct diet, they are advised to read Chapter 1 of this book.

With these clarifications and recommendations, now let me describe the asanas to be practised for curing the Spinal Pain. Begin your yoga practice as described below:

Yogic Treatment : First Week

During the first week, practice the following yoga *asanas:*

Pawan Mukta Asana: Lying position as described in Chapter 2.

Bhujanga Asana: Described in Chapter 2.

Shalabha Asana: With one leg, at a time as described in Chapter 2.

Uttanpada Asana: With one leg at a time as described in Chapter 2.

Shava Asana: For three minutes, as described in Chapter 2.

Second Week and Onwards

From the second week onwards, the order of yoga practice should be as mentioned below:

Pawan Mukta Asana: Lying position.

Bhujanga Asana: moderately and without any strain.

Shalabha Asana: With one leg, at a time.

Uttanpada Asana: With one leg at a time.

Ekpada Uttan Asana: As described in Chapter 4.

Rechaka-Puraka Pranayama: As described in Chapter 2.

Shava Asana: For three to seven minutes.

By following the recommendations on diet and on other aspects, and by the daily practise of yoga *asanas* listed above, you will be completely cured of all the disorders and pains in the neck and in the spinal regions without any medicinal aid.

9

Sinus And Headache

BOTH THESE disorders are related to the head. Whereas Sinus affects mainly the respiratory and the nasal passages, headache might be in different parts of the head. As such we are going to discuss these both together under this chapter. We will discuss first the Sinus problem.

SINUS

Sinus has become a very common disorder of the day. Millions suffer from this torturous problem all over the world. Its symptoms vary from case to case. There is excessive or constant sneezing, watering of the nose, blockage of one or both the nostrils, heaviness of head or headache. In some cases there could be one or many of the symptoms mentioned above. It makes the life of the patient miserable because of constant sneezing and at times due to complete congestion. Breathing becomes very difficult and the patient has to struggle for every breath. Due to regular blocking of the nose, voice is also affected. The chronic type of Sinus affects the voice badly.

In the medical sytem of treatment, Sinus is regarded as a

resultant state of allergy. Doctors try to find out the particular allergents to which the patient is allergic. Medicines and injections are given in accordance with the identified allergen for developing resistance in the patients. It is a very lengthy process and even then there is no certainty of curing the disorder.

I have found that though medicinal aids provide momentary relief, they do not provide any permanent cure to the patients. It is a common practice to advise the patients to avoid using or contacting certain popularly known allergents, such as certain spices, flowers, perfumes, smoke, certain plants, certain animals and countless other such things. At times it becomes very difficult to find out what allergent the individual is allergic to. The yogic system of treatment is very different from the medical system. Let me describe what we consider the causes and cure of this trouble.

Causes and Cure

From my experience in treating the patients of Sinus trouble at the Yoga Institute of Washington, U.S.A. and at the Indian Institute of Yoga, Patna, I have found that faulty diet is the primary cause of Sinus trouble. When an individual takes certian types of foods or things to drink in a regular way, they in due time, have a great conditioning effect upon the whole bodily system.

Those who keep taking such type of food or drink constantly, develop sensitivity in their body. As a result, some become more sensitive to certain types of allergents, whose reaction ultimately turns into Sinus. Let me eleborate this point.

Many people are in the habit of drinking water upon arising in the morning; some take water first, then tea or coffee; some take only coffee or tea. This drinking of tea or water on an empty stomach makes the bowel movement easy. But it has been found that such people develop greater sensitivity to various things of their daily use and also to the environment they live in. Then there are people who eat fried things most of the time. This also in due time affects the digestive system and creates greater sensitivity.

Some are in the habit of drinking milk either at the time of going to sleep during night or during other times of the day. Regular use of milk in heavy doses also causes sensitivity. When a person takes the above mentioned items regularly, sensitivity becomes greater and he or she gets affected by various types of allergents which first turn into allergy and later on take the form of Sinus.

In the yogic system of treatment, the main emphasis is on correcting the faulty diet. Patients are advised to take a balanced diet and to avoid certain items which are considered undesirable, unnecessary and unhealthy. They are recommended to eat only those foods which are considered good and healthy. The patient of Sinus should avoid the following items: (i) should stop taking bed-tea or drinking water after getting up in the morning; (ii) should not drink milk at any time, though certain milk preparations can be taken at times; (iii) should avoid using perfumes and hair oils with strong smell; (iv) should stop eating fried and roasted things; (v) should not eat butter or ghee regularly; and (vi) should stop using spices of sharp flavour or hot spices.

Diet chart for the patients of Sinus trouble is the same as recommended to patients of Abdominal Disorders in Chapter 2. The patients are advised to take their diet as described therein.

By taking the diet as recommended, and by following the *Pranayamas* recommended below, the patients should be cured of Sinus trouble within two to three weeks.

Yogic Treatment

Practice the following *Pranayamas* for curing Sinus disorder:

Rechaka-Puraka Pranayama: Described in chapter 2, see Fig. 1 and 2.

Bhastrika Pranayama: Described below

Shava Asana: Do for five minutes, as described in Chapter 2.

BHASTRIKA PRANAYAMA

The ideal time for practising the *Bhastrika Pranayama*

is in the morning, before breakfast. It is important to practise it when the stomach is empty. Those who would like to practise it in the evening or at some other time, must allow a gap of three to four hours after eating.

Position of Readiness

Be seated on some padded surface either in Lotus Pose or in *Sukha Asana* as shown in Fig. 1 and 2. Keep your head and spine erect. Keep your hands on your knees as shown in Fig. 48. Look directly in front and breathe normally. Keep the mouth closed. This is the position of readiness for *Bhastrika Pranayama*.

Steps for Practice

In this *Pranayama* the stomach is pulled inside and brought forward in a quick succession along with every inhalation and exhalation. While exhaling, the stomach is pulled inside and while inhaling, the stomach is pushed forward. It is done like the bellows of the blacksmith. In order to make the *Bhastrika Pranayama*, follow the steps described below:

(i)   During the first phase, start gradually and slowly exhale the air through both nostrils and at the same time start pulling the stomach inside. When you have exhaled the air fully, start inhaling and at the same time, start pushing the stomach forward. One exhalation and one inhalation make one unit of *Bhastrika Pranayama*.

(ii) After doing three or four units in a slow and gradual way, begin to breathe fast in quick successions. Make five to six inhalations and exhalations one after another rapidly during this second phase.

(iii) Then gradually slow down your speed. Breathe three to four times slowly in this last phase. Then rest for three to four normal breaths. Resting should take about twenty seconds. While resting, keep yoursef seated easily by relaxing the body either in the same position or sitting comfortably as you like.

160

(iv)   After resting for the desired period, repeat the
       Pranayama by following the same process as done
       during the first round.

Daily Practice

During the first week do two rounds only. From second
week onwards, do three to four rounds of *Bhastrika
Pranayama*. Do not ever do more than four rounds in a
single day.

Benefits

This *Pranayama* is unique in curing the troubles of the
respiratory system. It removes lung troubles and
congestion of the nasal passage. It is excellent for
removing any heart and chest ailments. It has effect on the
whole digestive sytem. It can be practised by people of any
age and sex.

HEADACHE

Of all the diseases prevalent in our society, headache (in
some form or the other) has become a common problem of
our time. It would not be out of place to mention that
perhaps no one is spared from this malady. Each one of us
has experienced a headache of some sort at some time in
our life. In the U.S.A. headache is so common amongst the
office working people that the pain relieving drugs are
always kept in bottles all the time and some of them take a
few tablets daily for getting rid of their headache.

People suffer from various types of headaches. Some
suffer from headaches for years together in a constant way.
Some are attacked by headache at certain times of the day
very often. In certain cases, there cold be pain in only half
of the forehead. The chronic type of headache is called
Migraine. There are various causes for headaches, a
comprehensive list of which is not easy to present. But
some of the well known causes of headache are given
below.

Causes

When the nervous system of the individual is strained

either due to internal or external strain and stress, one develops a headache. Head being the central place of all the nerves, any disorder which affects the nerves, consequently begins to show its impact on the central nervous system which results into head pain. This straining of the nerves can be due to various reasons, such as, high or low blood pressure, gastric trouble, constipation, wind problems, indigestion, sinus, eye pain or trouble, excessive smoking, use of tobacco in any form, excessive intake of coffee or tea, intake of alcoholic drinks, lack of proper rest and sleep, anxiety, tension and fatigue. Whatever be the cause or causes of headache, it is curable through yogic method of treatment in a permanent way. Let me describe the yogic way of curing this trouble.

Cure

The yogic method of treatment of headache is comprised of three aspects: (i) avoiding such items of daily use which strain the nerves; (ii) taking proper diet; and (iii) practising some selected *asanas, Pranayamas* and *Bandhas.*

Persons suffering from headache should not take more than two cups of tea or coffee in a day; should cut short or completely stop smoking and the use of tobacco in any form. Such alcoholic drinks should be stopped which cause 'hangover'. The patients should sleep for six to eight hours per day. should avoid being tense or angry, should live in such environment where plenty of fresh air is available. These are some essential precautions which need to be paid due attention for avoiding this pain.

The diet chart for patients of headache is the same as described in Chapter 2 (under the section Abdominal Disorder). It needs to be added that fruits, green vegetables, salad and any leafy vegetable should be taken daily together with other items of intake. They must not eat fried and roasted things. They should drink ten to fifteen glasses of fresh water every twenty-four hours, should eat lightly and avoid spices, specially of sharp flavour. By taking their diet according to the Diet Chart of Chapter 2, and by paying attention to the suggestions and recommendations made above, they should practise the following yogic exercises:

Yogic Treatment

Asanas, Pranayamas and *Bandhas* for curing headaches:
(1) *Suryanamaskar Asana:* Described in Chapter 2.
(2) *Bhujanga Asana:* Described in Chapter 2.
(3) *Jalandhar Bandha:* Described in Chapter 9.
(4) *Rechaka-Puraka* Pranayama:Described in Chapter 2.
(5) *Shitali Pranayama:* Described below)
(6) *Shava Asana:* Do for five to ten minutes at the end, as described in Chapter 2.

SHITALI PRANAYAMA

Shitali means cooling. It is a *pranayama* which cools the whole body. In this *pranayama,* air is inhaled through the mouth in slowly and constantly and exhaled through both the nostrils in the same way. This cools the whole body and at the same time relaxes the central nervous system. It is an easy *Pranayama* which can be performed by people of any age. Its method of practice is explained below.

Position of Readiness

Be seated either in *Padma Asana* or *Sukha Asana* as shown in Fig.2 and Fig.49. Bring your tongue forward to touch the teeth from inside. Open your lips slightly and lift the upper teeth a bit for a gap between upper and lowe teeth for sucking air as shown in Fig.49. Keep your spine and head straight. Close your eyes and be relaxed. This is the position of readinesss for *Shitali Pranayama.*

Steps for Practice

(i) Start inhaling air through the mouth in such a way that air is passed all over the tongue. Take as much air as you can comfortably.

(ii) Just when the inhaling is over, start exhaling the air through the nostrils slowly and constantly and throw out all the air.

(iii) Just when exhaling is over, start inhaling through the mouth and between the teeth and exhaling through the nostrils continuously. One inhaling and one exhaling make one round. Do this for ten rounds.

(iv) After doing ten rounds of this *pranayama*, rest for about thirty seconds. During the rest, keep your mouth closed and breathe normally. Feel the cooling effect of the *pranayama* in the mouth, throat, head and also all over the body. After resting for the desired period make ten more rounds in the same way as during the first round of practice.

Daily practice

Do twenty to thirty rounds of this *pranayama* daily in units of ten at a time, and rest for thirty seconds after every ten units as described above. It is important that while resting, keep your mouth closed and keep breathing normally. Do not talk while resting. Silence while resting will have greater effect of cooling on the nerves all over the body.

Benefits

It has a great energising, soothing, relaxing and cooling effect on all the nerve channels and on the whole body. People suffering from high blood pressure, gastric troubles, tension and anxiety will find this very effective in removing these disorders.

In yogic literature it is said that if one feels thirsty or hungry at a place where water and food are not available, this *pranayama* satisfies both thirst and hunger. Since this *pranayama* has a great cooling effect on the system it is just possible that some practitioners may catch cold or get a sore throat by practising it. If this happens, they are advised to gargle with hot saline water. This gargling with salted water will remove the cold caused due to *Shitali*.

Fig 37   Veera Asana

Fig 38 Gomukh Asana

Fig 39 Vriksha Asana

Fig 40   Setubandha Asana

Fig 41   Siddha Asana

Fig 42   Natraj Asana

Fig 43 Manduka Asana

Fig 44   Hala Asana (easy pose)

Fig 45   Hala Asana

Fig 46 Practice of Concentration

10

Eye Disorders

UNDER THIS chapter we are going to describe the yogic method of curing certain eye defects concerned specifically with visionary power. It needs to be stated that the 'yogic method of cure' is not applied for correcting the organic defects, such as, Cataract, Glaucoma and other disorders of this nature. These defects have to be treated by the eye specialists. But in those cases where surgical treatment is not necessary, disorders like eye strains, eye pain, diminishing visionary power, near and far sightedness and other visionary defects can be cured through the yogic system. Further, the problems like watering of the eyes, itching in the region of the eyes, blurring of the vision, redness in one or both the eyes can easily be cured through the yogic method. In other words, the defects which do not require any surgery and are considered curable through medicinal aids, can be cured through yoga without use of any medicines.

Disorders of the eye. affecting especially the visionary power are becoming an alarming problem all over the world. The problem is more acute in the developing countries than in the advanced ones. One immediate cause for this deterioration in visionary power is related to malnutrition. We know that millions cannot afford to have proper diet which affects the health and ultimately the visionary power is also affected. Though the individual is quite normal and free from diseases, due to lack of proper nourishment, his health and the power of his eyes become gradually weak. Consequently, even when there is no specific disease in the eyes, the deterioration of the visionary power continues. First let me point out the causes of these eye troubles.

Causes

When every thing is normal but one still develops some eye disorder of non-organic type, it is mainly due to faulty diet and certain undesirable habits. For example, many have the habit of eating mostly fried, highly spiced and seasoned food. Some develop the habit of drinking excessive coffee, tea or hard liquor; smoking excessively; lack of rest or sleep; and undue straining of the eyes. There are three categories of the sufferers in this respect:

(i) those who can afford but are in the habit of eating only a particular type of food which causes malnutrition;

(ii) those who are financially weak and cannot afford to eat a balanced diet; and (iii) those who suffer from certain identified undesirable habits. The patients of all these three categories can correct their eye defects with only a little attention and care.

Cure

Patients suffering from any disorder of the visionary power need to pay special attention to diet and correcting certain habits. They *must stop* eating things which are harmful to the visionary power of the eyes; and they *should* eat those things which are conducive to the growth and restoration of the visionary power.

Yogic Treatment

Suryanamaskar Asana: (Described in Ch. 3).
Trikona Asana: (Described in Ch. 5).

Bhujanga Asana: (Described in Ch. 2).
Yoga Mudra: (Described in Ch. 4).
Jalandhar Bandh:(Described in Ch. 9).
Shava Asana: (Described in Ch. 2).
Eye Exercises: (Described below).

It is advised to practise yoga *asanas* in the same order as they are listed above. At the end of the yoga practice, one should rest in *Shava Asana* for about five minutes. When the *Shava Asana* is over, the eye exercises should be practised.

EYE EXERCISES

We are going to describe two types of Eye Exercises. They are classified as Exercise A and Exercise B. We will discuss first the exercise of Group 'A'.

Eye Exercise-'A'

In this exercise you are going to make eye movements without making any movement of the head and neck. You have to keep your head, neck and spine erect and move only the eyes as directed. Do not pull your eyes excessively in any direction. Make the movement without any excessive strain on the eyes. Try to develop a rhythm in the movement of the eyes. With this understanding begin your practice as described below:

(i)   Be seated in *Sukha Asana* (easy pose). Keep the spine, neck and head straight in one line. Look directly in front at the level of your eyes. Breathe normally. This is the position of readiness.

(ii) Move your eyes upwards towards the sky or ceiling. Stay there for two seconds. Then look downward towards the earth and stay there for two seconds. Again look towards the sky and after staying there for two seconds, look downwards and stay there for two seconds. Do this upward and downward movement twice. This makes one unit of the exercise. After doing this, close your eyes for two seconds.

(iii) Then open your eyes and look in front. Now look towards the right side and try to see as far as you can. Then look towards the left side and stay there for two seconds and try to see as far as possible. Then look again to the right side. Then go to the left side. Now look in front again. Close your eyes. One unit of this left-right exercise is over. Keep your eyes closed for six to eight seconds.

Note: Remember that one unit of up-down movement plus one unit of right-left movement are counted together as one round of this eye exercise. When one round is over rest for six to eight seconds. After resting for a few seconds, make two more rounds of this up-down and left-right exercise. As one practise this exercise one unconsciously learns how to practise eye movements systematically.

Daily Practice

During the first week, do two rounds daily. From the second week onwards, do three to four rounds daily. After doing the desired rounds, do the palming as suggested below:

Palming

Rub your palms against one another so that heat is generated in the palms by this friction. After rubbing the palms thus for six to eight seconds, place the left palm on the left eye and the right palm on the right eye, as shown in Fig.50. When you place the palms on the eyes, no pressure should be felt on the eyes. They should be lightly pressed on the outer part of the eye region. When the palms cover the eyes, keep them there for eight to ten seconds.

After eight to ten seconds, remove the palms and rest. This completes one round of palming. After resting for six to eight seconds, do two more rounds of palming, as you did during the first time. When the palming is over you are free to do anything you wish. You can add the following eye exercise of Group 'B' from the second week onward.

Eye Exercise-'B'

In this exercise you move the eyes in a clockwise and

anticlockwise motion. When the movement is according to the movement of the arms of the clock, it is called clockwise and when the movement is reversed it is called anticlockwise.

For doing this Group 'B' exercise, follow the steps as described below:

(i) Look straight in front. Lift your eyes up and start moving them in a circular way, coming to the right side and then going down, then to the left side and then upward again. This makes one unit of clockwise exercise. Repeat this twice and rest for six to eight seconds. While resting, keep your eyes closed.

(ii) Now you are going to do the anticlockwise movement of the eyes. Look in front of you. Then look upward towards the ceiling, then to the left side, then downward, then come to the right side, then upward again in a circular way. This makes one anticlockwise movement of the eyes. Continue this to make the movement twice. This makes one unit of the anticlockwise movement. Now rest for six to eight seconds. While resting, keep the eyes closed.

One unit of clockwise and one unit of anticlockwise exercise makes one round of this 'B' exercise. Do this clockwise and anticlockwise exercise for two rounds and then rest for ten seconds by closing your eyes. After resting is over, do the palming for three to four times. After palming, your exercise is over.

Daily Practice

From the second week onward, first practice four rounds of Group 'A'. Then do four rounds of Group 'B'. After completing the exercise of Group A and B, do four rounds of palming at the end.

This eye exercise can be practised twice independently within twenty-four hours. It means you can do only the eye exercises without doing yoga. Those practising twice should give a gap of eight hours between the first and the second session.

177

Proper Diet

Patients should not eat fatty, fried, roasted and hard to digest eatables. They should stop taking meat, chicken highly seasoned or spicy food. They should avoid eating pickles, red pepper and other items which strain the nerves. They should not take coffee and tea Use of tobacco in any form and smoking should be stopped.

What to Eat

The main consideration in their diet should be on a balanced diet. Having a balanced diet depends more on making efforts than on spending money. It does not cost much to have all the ingredients of a balanced diet. The primary consideration is to include salad, green vegetables, leafy vegetables and fruits of any kind in your daily intake. They should take their food according to the diet chart given below:

Breakfast (7 to 9 A.M.)

(i)	Orange juice or any fruit juice	-one cup
	or sweet orange or *mausami*	-one
(ii)	Fresh apple or any fresh fruit	-one or as desired.
(iii)	Wheat bread with green vegetables	-as desired.
(iv)	Germinated gram (two days old)	-¼ cup or in desired quantity
(v)	Milk or Ovaltine	-one cup to one glass

Lunch and Dinner (12 to 2 P.M.,6 to 8 P.M.)

(i)	Salad (a mixture of tomato, cucumber, radish, lettuce, cabbage, carrot, etc. with very little salt and lemon juice or with fresh dressing or plain)	-one cup
(ii)	Vegetable soup	-one cup
(iii)	Wheat bread *(Chapati)*	-as desired
(iv)	Pulse (*Moong, Masur, Chana* or Green Peas)	-as desired

(v)	*Saag* (leafy vegetable of any kind)	-as desired
(vi)	Green vegetable (of any kind)	-as desired
(vii)	Fish or Liver (for non-vegetarians)	-on alternate days

Afternoon Refreshment (3 to 5 P.M.)

(i)	Fresh fruit of any type	-as desired
(ii)	Salted Biscuits or *chana ghughani* or *sattu* or milk pudding of bread	-as desired
(iii)	Ovaltine or Bournvita	-one cup

The important point to be kept in mind is that major course of your daily diet should be salad, fresh fruits and green vegetables. Food should be cooked in vegetable oils with no spices or very little of it. Special attention should be paid in observing the following principles while eating:

Principles and Requirement of Eating

(i) To eat slowly after chewing the food very thoroughly.

(ii) To eat (specially dinner) at least two hours prior to sleeping time at night.

(iii) Never eat more than 85 per cent of your capacity at any time. In other words, always eat a little less than you need.

(iv) Avoid drinking water while eating. Drink water after half an hour of eating, take ten to fifteen glasses of fresh water every twenty-four hours.

By following the principles and method of eating as described above and by practising yoga asanas daily you can certainly cure your eye problems.

11

Heart Ailments And High Blood Pressure

MILLIONS OF people in the world suffer from the diseases of the heart and blood vessels, which are called 'Cardiovascular Diseases'. It has already become 'the number one killer disease' in the developed countries like the U.S.A. and Western Europe. It is also on frightening increase in the developing countries. According to the American Medical Association, more than fifty per cent of all the deaths in the United States every year are caused due to cardiovascular diseases and it is now called 'the epidemic of the 20th century'.[1]

Therefore, it appears very important to know what these cardiovascular diseases are; what are their causing factors; and how these diseases can be controlled, cured and prevented through therapeutic yoga. Since these diseases

---

[1]See, American Medical Association, *Today's Health Guide* (U.S.A., : A.M.A., 1968), p. 380.

are related to the heart and the blood vessels, some basic understanding of these oragans appears essential.

The heart is a tough muscular pump whose constant function is to eject blood to the arterial system at an average rate 70 to 75 times per minute. The heart keeps the blood circulation going by receiving it in its chambers from every part of the body through the veinous system, and then by pumping it out to all parts of the body through the arteries. It is a complicated mechanism which breaks down at times in many individuals.

When any part of the circulatory system does not receive the needed blood supply, it gets damaged. This damage could be in the heart itself or in any other parts, such as, the lungs, the kidneys, the brain and other organs. Due to any breakdown in this mechanism in the heart, there is heart ailment or heart attack, as commonly called.

The diseases associated with cardiovascular system, which can be treated through therapeutic yoga, are the following: atherosclerosis (hardening of the arteries), coronary thrombosis (sudden blocking of the arteries of the heart), and degenerative heart diseases, and hypertensive diseases. Let me describe briefly what these diseases are:

Atherosclerosis

The inner walls of the arteries get thickened due to gradual deposits of fatty material. These gradual deposits take the form of layers in the inner walls of the arteries and, as a result, there is hindrance to the flow of blood. Consequently, blood clotting occurs in the roughened areas and the blood circulation gets blocked.

Coronary Thrombosis

There is a *sudden blocking* of one of the arteries or its branches and then the supply of blood to the heart is affected partially or wholly. The sudden blocking takes place due to the deposit of clot in an already narrow artery. Due to lack of blood supply, heart attack takes place with pain in the chest and arms and there may be perspiration.

Degenerative Heart Disease

It occurs due to gradual decay of the blood vessels. It is thought that excessive smoking of tobacco in any form causes degeneration of the blood vessels.[2] The degenerative disease generally occurs among the middle-aged and the elderly persons. In his case, though the heart muscle continues to work, it does not possess enough strength to maintain the needed healthy function.

Hypertensive Heart Disease

It occurs due to constant presence of high blood pressure in an individual. When the blood pressure continues to remain very high, it overstrains the heart muscles and also the whole of the circulatory system. This overstraining causes wear and tear of the tissues, leads to the hardening of the blood vessels, and diminishes supply of blood to the heart and brain. Sometimes, the supply of blood to the brain gets so diminished that paralysis of one or both sides of the body occurs.

It is now commonly accepted that a major cause of cardiovascular ailments is due to psychosomatic factors. The illness resulting from strain and stress is now known as psychosomatic (the word being comprised of two Greek words, *psyche* and *soma*, which mean mind and body).

The most common strain and stress are due to nervousness, which arise because of fear, anxiety, apprehension, tension and restlessness, anger, jealousy, frustration and various other such feelings.

It is held in yoga that the mind controls, governs and activates the body. Body in this sense becomes a tool of the mind. What happens is that the mind-straining factors begin to strain also the bodily systems. Most of the diseases of our time, such as, the heart ailments, hypertension, asthma, and others are mostly related to these mental strain and stress which are called in medical term 'psychosomatic factors'.

---

[2]See, Dr. Alice Chase, *Nutrition for Health* (New York, Parker Publishing Company, 1967), p. 68.

Since this chapter covers Heart Ailments and High Blood Pressure both, it would be proper to describe the latter in brief before recommending their yogic treatment.

High Blood Pressure

In a normal and healthy person the blood pressure remains 120 systolic and 80 diastolic. But when there are abnormalities in the arteries or in the circulatory system, the systolic pressure rises very high and at times, diastolic also rises.

The rise in the pressure is caused due to the narrowness in the arteries, the heart has to work harder for pushing the blood through them and as a result of which there is high blood pressure, and in medical terms this is called 'hypertension'.

Though it is normal for the blood pressure to rise high during excitement and at certain emotional moments, but it goes down shortly. Such rises do not cause any harmful effect. But when blood pressure continues to remain excessively high it causes various disorders, such as, lack of strength, tiredness, headache, and at times, difficulty in breathing, bad temper, visionary troubles, and coldness in the hands and feet.

It is now a medically established fact that hypertension may at times be due to psychosomatic factors. It could also be due to advancing age and thereby due to degenerative factors (already discussed earlier). In the following pages, process of treatment for hypertension as well as for heart is now described:

Yogic Treatment

It does not need to be emphasized that therapeutic yoga is not a treatment for an emergency case of heart attack on severe hypertension. Therapeutic yoga should be practised when the individual concerned is not affected by an emergency type of condition.

In our treatment at the Indian Institute of Yoga, Patna, we have found that the patients of heart ailments have regained their normal health within two to three months of yoga practice. Further, once the restoration of health has been achieved, the patients remain in good health without any complaint. Likewise, in cases of high blood pressure, we have found that normalization of circulatory system occurs within one to two months when the patient has been cooperative in following out instructions.

It is significant to mention that yogic system of treatment is the same for heart ailments as for hypertension. The treatment is comprised of three steps (i) observance to certain principles and advice, (ii) eating proper diet, and (iii) practising yoga on selected basis. Let me explain first some important principles and advice.

Principles and Advice

They should stop smoking cigarettes and use of tobacco in any form, and should give up taking tea and coffee. Alcoholic drinks should be discontinued. Intake of *ghee* butter, cream, eggs, meat, excessive fat containing food items should be stopped.

Note: Hot spices, pickles, chutney, red chillies, and excessive use of salt should be excluded from the eating items. Must avoid over eating at all times. Must stop late hour working and keeping awake longer during night. Such precautions would prevent the ailments.

For a detailed understanding about diet, bathing, cleaning, and other yogic principles, the users of this section are advised to read thoroughly the First Chapter of this book. Some important advice which are not covered in the first chapter, are mentioned below:

One major advice is to be relaxed and keep yourself free from anxiety, nervousness, tension and restlessness. Though it is not easy for every individual to be relaxed in every condition and situation, it can be done with proper understanding about 'Self, Society and the Nature'. These aspects are discussed in Chapter 7 of this book and you are

184

Fig 47 Jalandhar Bandha

Fig 48   Bhastrika Pranayama

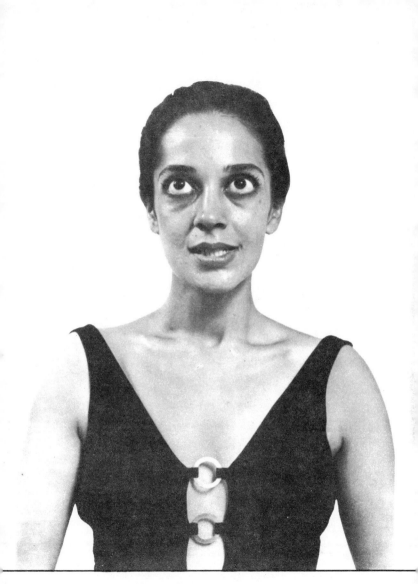

Fig 49   Shitali Pranayama

Fig 50 Palming the Eye

advised to read it properly for developing self-power for overcoming these tension-creating problems.[3]

Yoga practice

The patients of heart ailments and hypertension should practise yoga, in phases, according to the guidelines given below:

First Phase

It should last for three weeks. In this phase, only *Shava Asana* needs to be practised. A detailed description about the method of practising *Shava Asana* is given in Chapter 2. The practitioner should first read and develop a proper understanding about the process of *Shava Asana* before actually practising it. One important advice is that do not practise it in a hurry. Do it thoroughly and with patience. Be quite at ease when you practise *Shava Asana* .

Daily Practice

Shava Asana should be practised twice or thrice daily. At one stretch, it should be performed for about thirty to forty minutes. Best suitable times for practising it, are in the morning (before breakfast), in the afternoon (2 hours after lunch) and in the evening. The main consideration is that stomach should be empty and not heavy with food while practising *Shava Asana*.

Those suffering from high blood pressure should get themselves examined to find out their condition after practising *Shava Asana* for three weeks. By this time, blood pressure should definitely be normalized. When the blood pressure becomes normal, they should add the *asanas* of the second and the third phase described below. But in case, the blood pressure remains more than 150 systolic, they should keep practising only *Shava Asana*, till normalization comes.

[3]Those interested in further reading are advised to see Dr. Phulgenda Sinha, *Yoga: Meaning, Values and Practice* (Patna: Indian Institute of Yoga, 1970), pp. 32-72.

Benefits

Though the benefits of *Shava Asana* are already mentioned in Chapter 2 a few words need to be added here. Our experience shows that a regular and proper practise of *Shava Asana* for about two to three weeks brings a remarkable good effect on the patients of heart ailments and of high blood pressure. It corrects the disorders of the circulatory system by relaxing the nerves and the internal organs. Because of normalizing and relaxing effect on the arteries, high blood pressure is reduced and gradually it is corrected.

Second Phase (Fourth and Fifth Weeks)

Before practising Yoga of this phase, the practitioner must read 'Essentials of Yoga Practice' as described in Chapter 1 with special attention to the requirements of rest. After practising *Shava Asana* twice or thrice daily during the First Phase, the following *asanas* should be added. Now Yoga practice should be in the numerical order listed below:

(i) *Pawanmukta Asana:* (in lying position): It is comprehensively described in Chapter 2. Practise it without straining yourself. Do only as much as you can make comfortably. Make four to six rounds daily.

(ii) *Uttanpada Asana:* (with only one leg at a time. It is fully described in Chapter 2. In the beginning, hold the leg up for only a few seconds. Gradually increase the time to four, then to six seconds. Daily practice should be only six rounds (three rounds with each leg).

(iii) *Shava Asana:* When other *asanas* are practised, *Shava Asana* should be done at the end. Method of practising *Shava Asana* remains the same as followed during the first phase. Duration of *Shava Asana* when done after Yoga practice, may be reduced if so desired. A practise of fifteen to thirty minutes should be sufficient.

During this second phase, *Shava Asana* should continue to be practised singly also, at least one more time during a period of twenty-four hours.

Third Phase (Sixth Week Onwards)

During this phase and onward, the daily practice of Yoga should be in the following order:

(i) *Pranayama* (with *Rechaka* and *Puraka*) Its method of practice is well illustrated and described in Chapter 2. Practise according to the directions given therein.

(ii) *Suryanamaskar Asana:* As described in Chapter 3.

(iii) *Santulan Asana:* As described in Chapter 5.

(iv) *Pawanmukta Asana:* As done earlier.

(v) *Uttanpada Asana:* As done earlier.

(vi) *Shava Asana:* As done earlier.

Diet Chart

Breakfast (7 to 9 A.M.)

(i) Orange juice or any fruit juice or sweet orange or *mausammi* — one cup / -one

(ii) Fresh apple or any fresh fruit (except mangoes and *lichi*) — one or as / -desired

(iii) Germinated gram (of two days) — ¼ cup

(iv) Wheat bread with green vegetables or toast — as desired

(v) Skimmed milk (if desired) — one cup

Lunch and Dinner (12 to 2 P.M., 6 to 8 P.M.)

(i) Salad (a) mixture of tomato, cucumber, radish, lettuce, carrot etc., with very little salt and lemon juice or with french dressing or plain — one cup

(ii) Vegetable soup — one cup

(iii) Wheat bread (*chapati*) — as desired

(iv) Pulse (*moong, masur, chana,* or green peas) — as desired

(v) *Saag* (leafy vegetables of any kind) — as desired

(vi) Green vegetables (of any kind) — as desired

Fish (for non-vegetarians) — 2 moderate pieces on alternate days

Afternoon Refreshment (3 to 5 P.M.)

(i) Fresh fruit of any type   -as desired

(ii) Salted biscuits or *chana ghughani*   -as desired

The important points to be kept in mind are that major part of every day diet should be of salad, fresh fruits and green vegetables. Dishes should be cooked in vegetable oils by using no spices or very little of it.

12

Yoga For Good Health

SINCE THE first publication of this book, I have received numerous letters of appreciation from every part of India and also from other countries. A great number of patients who have been cured from their chronic diseases through this book have requested me to suggest yoga asanas they should practice daily for maintaining good health and for preventing recurrence of their disorders. In accordance with those requests, a chart of yoga practice is presented herewith.

The chart is so made that it will be beneficial to all those practitioners who have been cured from certain disorders as well as to those who wish to practise yoga for physical fitness purposes. The practitioners will have two distinct benefits by performing the asanas of this chart. (i) it will prevent recurrence of the disorders they had been suffering from; and (ii) a regular yoga practice will keep them in sound physical and mental health.

In this chart, the *asanas* and *pranayamas* have been divided into several groups according to their nature and bodily impact. The practitioners should select one or two *asanas* from each group according to their preference and liking. The *asanas* from Group 1 to 5 are easy and can be performed by persons of any age and any physical condition. The *asanas* of Group 6 are a little difficult and it may not be possible for every one to practise them. It is advised that those who can not practise *asanas* of Group 6 should make their selection of *asanas* from other group and they would not be missing anything. The practice of yoga should be made on the basis of personal convenience, suitability of time, body condition etc. of the practitioners. A regular practise of fifteen minutes per day or at least five days in a week would show excellent result to the practitioners.

A special advice is that when you practice Yoga even for ten or fifteen minutes, you must do *Shava Asana*, at the end. For the details of *Shava Asana*, please read Ch. 1 and Ch. 2. Those who would like to practise Eye exercises, Concentration and Meditation, should practise after the *Shava Asana*. The practitioners are advised to see the respective figures and pages of their selection for practising them.

With these clarifications, the chart is listed below:

Group I

Suryanamaskar Asana: two to four rounds: See Chapter 2.

Santulan Asana: two to four rounds: See Chapter 5.

Pawanmukta Asana: four rounds: See Chapter 2.

Ujjayee Pranayama: five rounds in standing or in lying position: See Chapter 4.

Rechaka-Puraka Pranayama: ten rounds as described in Chapter 2.

Bhastrika Pranayama: ten rounds as described in Chapter 10.

Group III

Trikona Asana: four rounds: See Chapter 5.

Tara Asana: two to four rounds: See Chapter 4.

Ardhavakra Asana: two to four rounds: See Chapter 3.

Group IV

Bhujanga Asana: two to four rounds: See Chapter 2.
Shalabha Asana: two to four rounds to be practised after *Bhujanga Asana:* See Chapter 2.
Paschimottan Asana: two to four rounds: See Chapter 2.
Uttanpada Asana: two to four rounds: See Chapter 2.
Ekpada Uttan Asana: two to four rounds: See Chapter 4.

Group V

Veera Asana: four rounds: See Chapter 5.
Vriksha Asana: four rounds: See Chapter 5.
Gomukha Asana: four rounds: See Chapter 5.
Yoga Mudra: two to four rounds: See Chapter 4.

Group VI

Sarvanga Asana: one to three minutes: See Chapter 4.
Matsya Asana: two rounds, to be practised after *Sarvanga Asana:* See Chapter 4.
Hala Asana: two to four rounds: See Chapter 7.
Dhanur Asana: two to four rounds: See Chapter 3.

General

Shava Asana: for 1/4 of Yoga practising time at the end: See Chapter 2.
Eye Exercise: (as described in Ch. 11)
Practice of Concentration and Meditation (if desired: See Chapter 7).

Select Bibliography

Early Period
Gherand Samhita
Goraksha Paddhati
Hatha Pradipika
Samkhya Darshan by Kapil
Vasistha Samhita
Yoga Sutra by Patanjali

Modern Period

Acharya Bhadrasen, *Yoga Aur Swasthya* (Ajmer: Adarsha Sahitya Niketan, 1951).

Dr. Phulgenda Sinha, *Yoga: Meaning, Values and Practice* (Patna: Indian Institute of Yoga, 1970).

Swami Kuvalayananda, *Pranayama* (Bombay: Popular Prakashan, 1972).

Swami Kuvalayananda, *Yogasana* (Bombay: Popular Prakashan, 1965).

Swami Sivananda, *Yoga Asanas* (India: The Divine Life Society, 1972).

Swami Sivananda, *Thought Power* (India: The Divine Life Society, 1970).

Swami Vivekananda, *Jnana Yoga* (India: Ramakrishna Mission).

Swami Vivekananda, *Karma Yoga* (India: Ramakrishna Mission).

Swami Vivekananda, *Raja Yoga* (India: Ramakrishna Mission).